MIND PUMP

The Psychology of Bodybuilding

D1124761

Tom Kubistant, EdD
Performance and Productivity Specialists, Inc.
Reno, Nevada

Leisure Press
Champaign, Illinois

Library of Congress Cataloging-in-Publication Data

Kubistant, Tom, 1950–
    Mind pump.

    Bibliography: p.
    Includes index.
    1. Bodybuilding—Psychological aspects.
2. Physical fitness—Psychological aspects.
I. Title.
GV546.5.K82   1988   646.7'5   87-17345
ISBN 0-88011-296-4 (pbk.)

Developmental Editor: Judy Patterson Wright, PhD
Production Director: Ernie Noa
Projects Manager: Lezli Harris
Copy Editors: Linda Barr and Lise Rodgers
Assistant Editor: JoAnne Cline
Proofreader: Linda Purcell
Typesetter: Brad Colson
Text and Cover Design: Keith Blomberg
Text Layout: Denise Mueller
Printed By: Versa Press, Inc.
Cover Photo: Bill Morrow
Interior Photography: Wilmer Zehr, Lenore Morrison, Ernie Noa,
    and Diane Schultz

ISBN: 0-88011-296-4

Copyright © 1988 by Tom Kubistant, EdD

Printed in the United States of America

10 9 8 7 6 5 4 3 2 1

Leisure Press
A division of Human Kinetics Publishers, Inc.
Box 5076, Champaign, IL 61820
1-800-DIAL-HKP
1-800-334-3665 (in Illinois)

To Carrie,
My Love.

Acknowledgments

There are some special people I would like to thank for their help with this book. I think it is important to acknowledge them so they can receive the recognition they deserve.

—To Rainer Martens of Human Kinetics Publishers for his ongoing support of this book.
—To Dr. Judy Patterson Wright, my developmental editor, for her tireless dedication, commitment, and enthusiasm for this project. She made a difference.
—To Mike Mentzer for his intelligent input and inspiration. He is "The Thinking Person's Bodybuilder."
—To Joe Weider for not only his continued support of me, but also his promotion of the mental components of bodybuilding. "The Master Blaster" really is the patriarch of this sport.
—To Rhonda Lenon for her manuscript typing services.
—To our photographic team: Wilmer Zehr, Photographer and Keith Blomberg, Photo Shoot Director.
—To our models: Debra Facer, Jeff Facer, Miriam Millikin, Tim Thompson, Kristi Wilkin, Brett Thompson, Stacey Travers, Robert Walters, and Kevin Masi.
—To Dan Crawmer, manager of the Omni Fitness Center, Champaign, Illinois, for his help with our auditioning process.
—To Bill Kroll, Head Strength Coach, University of Illinois, Champaign, Illinois, for his help with our photographic location.
—To Kevin Noble, Contest Director, AAU Bodybuilding Championships, Elgin, Illinois, November 1, 1986, for his help with our competition photographs.
—And to all the bodybuilders with whom I have worked and from whom I have learned, so that I could share these insights with others.

Contents

Preface

*E*arly morning tennis practice for our college team was, indeed, early morning. The only time we could use the indoor tennis courts was between midnight and 3:00 a.m. So Sunday through Thursday we would practice and play intrasquad matches while our friends would be peacefully sleeping. It would be one of those nights that would change my life and, ultimately, take me into a new fitness dimension.

During one of these early morning practices a sickening crack echoed through the air of the tennis courts. It was a crack that was far louder than any booming cannonball serve. Everyone stopped, because even though their brains did not immediately know what this sound was, their stomachs did. My knee had literally exploded.

Lying in the hospital bed after the operation, I had my orthopedic surgeon tell me that it was a very major surgery; the cartilage was crumbled and I had only a couple of strands of ligaments remaining on the outside of the knee. Now, this was back in the Dark Ages of orthopedic surgery when they seemed to use chainsaws and Black & Decker drills to get the job done! So any such operation required major rehabilitation.

I learned that much of the rehabilitation consisted of lifting weights in order to strengthen the atrophied muscles around the damaged knee. One morning I was wheeled down to the physical therapy room (for some reason, they are always in the basement of hospitals) where I was confronted with a strange array of machines. It looked like a modern-day chamber of horrors! I saw other patients working out with obvious discomfort and even pain. But I also observed them exhibiting more determination and sheer guts than I had ever seen on the faces of my elite athlete friends. I also saw, but could not comprehend at that time, that these people seemed to feel a great deal of pride and satisfaction in what they were doing. It was indeed a strange place.

When it was my turn to work, I was inundated with such foreign terminology as "reps," "sets," "leg extensions," and "leg curls." The exercises were excruciatingly uncomfortable and even scary, but there was no other choice than to do them. Although I was unaware of it at the time, this was my introduction to the world of bodybuilding.

Throughout the subsequent weeks, with the help of the weights, I made steady progress. The shriveled quadriceps and hamstrings started to improve in strength, endurance, and even size. The once-strange machines now became friends. I set goals for each session, concentrated as I had never done before, persisted, and succeeded. I also started feeling the pride and satisfaction that I had sensed that first day in the gym.

Then came a day when I observed that my "bad" leg's muscles were stronger and larger than my "good" leg's. So I had to start working out my other leg to bring it up to the new standard of my operated leg. Deep down inside me I knew I was extending my body further than I had ever done before. However, I experienced that I was also extending my mind further than I had ever done before as well.

Finally, there came a day when I realized my new commitment to bodybuilding. I said to myself, "Look at how much I have improved both legs. I don't need lifting weights anymore to rehabilitate myself. But I want to lift weights to see just how far I can develop my entire body."

That was the day I became a bodybuilder.

The Explosion

There has been an explosion. This explosion is not in the population rate or even one of those occurring at the Nevada Nuclear Test Site. It is an explosion that is happening quietly on the running paths and rhythmically in the swimming pools. It occurs during lonely early morning sit-ups or in a crowded aerobics studio. It goes on in the expanses of a bicycle tour or in the confines of a racquetball court.

The explosion is fitness.

Thousands of people every week are rediscovering—or perhaps discovering for the first time—the joys of movement, flexibility, endurance, and strength. What begins as impossible tasks and challenges eventually becomes easy and even fun.

As we get into better shape, we may ask ourselves a related question. "If these exercises brought me into shape, just how far can I go in promoting my fitness?" The answer suggests that in order to really develop the body there needs to be more resistance than just bodyweight, time, or gravity. There need to be weights.

Whether people use weight training as a supplemental strength-increasing activity for another sport or use it for its own sake, women and men are discovering the joys of "pumping iron." They are coming together from all walks of life to share a common bond: melding iron with muscle.

As more people experience the results and joys of bodybuilding, the old stereotypes and prejudices about the sport are falling by the wayside. Bodybuilders are not "ironheads" who do not possess any intelligence. They are not "narcissists" who are self-centered just because they look at themselves in a mirror. Women are not "unfeminine" because they develop muscle that was once thought to be exclusively a man's domain. Bodybuilders are not "gym rats" who do not have anything better to do with their lives. And most importantly, they are not "freaks" or "aberrations."

What bodybuilders *are*, are representatives of a leading edge of fitness. They push their bodies into becoming realities of what artists throughout the centuries could create only on canvas or with clay or marble. Bodybuilders are becoming models of what can be done with the human body.

The Missing Key

Along with the explosion in the popularity of bodybuilding has come an explosion in training techniques and approaches, nutrition, sports medicine, exercise physiology, and even advances in tanning and skin care. While this plethora of information may temporarily confuse some beginning bodybuilders, it can eventually facilitate better gains.

However, there is one factor in bodybuilding that has been all but ignored. It is a key that successful bodybuilders have acquired to unlock their potential and accelerate their development. What is this missing key? It is not a new machine, nutritional supplement, or even a training technique.

It is the mind.

As progressive and innovative as bodybuilding is, it has still not adequately addressed how the mind can promote physical growth and development. Occasionally a training book includes a chapter about the mental side of bodybuilding, but it is usually limited to contest preparation and competition. No comprehensive and systematic exploration into the psychology of bodybuilding has ever been undertaken.

This is what this book is all about. It presents a clear and complete approach into how the mind can be used in aiding development of the body. It combines state-of-the-art knowledge from the leading edges of such fields as psychology, exercise physiology, holistic health, sports medicine, and even quantum physics. This book presents the information in such a way that it can be easily applied to daily training sessions.

This book is for all levels of bodybuilders—from the novice to the Ms. and Mr. Olympia contender—who wish to maximize their workouts and progress. This book can be used by novice body-builders who are still unfamiliar with the types of exercises and equipment, people who want to get into better shape, people who need to rehabilitate and strengthen injured body parts, intermediate

bodybuilders who want to sculpt their bodies to match their dreams, advanced bodybuilders who want an effective way to refine their developments, and competitive bodybuilders who want to learn how to present themselves better and gain an edge over their opposition. In short, this book is for any person who trains with weights and wants to learn to better coordinate the mind and the body.

How to Use This Book

This book explores the major components in effectively applying the mind in pumping iron. It presents a complete and usable system of mental training that is both easily understood and easily adaptable. It offers a step-by-step program that blends proven theory with practical application.

The best way to read this book is in the sequence it is written. If you are having a specific problem that one of the later chapters addresses, go ahead and read that chapter, but then read the entire book from the beginning. In order for any one topic to make complete sense, you must develop the overall perspective provided by the earlier chapters. The system of Mind Pump is dependent on following the sequence of chapters.

Each chapter is constructed to present the information in clear, concise, and practical ways. It is written to stimulate you to think. Every chapter has many examples, self-assessments, and guidelines to help you better learn the material. At the end of each chapter is a summary of that part of the system of mental training that you can apply to your daily workouts.

If you own this book, mark in it and write notes in it or in a record like your training log. The physical act of writing something down lends itself to better retention of that information and promotes more commitment in applying it. I want you to be an active participant in this book.

As you read this book, I would like you to ask yourself continuously, ''Now, how can I apply this specific point to my training?'' The information in this book is designed for you to use or practice. If you do not apply this information, you have wasted your time and money. Information without implementation leads to confusion and, eventually, to stagnation. Learning something implies *doing* something with it. So continually focus on how you can apply these concepts to your training.

When we read self-help books, we frequently have a tendency to become overwhelmed with all the material presented. What usually happens is that we try to apply all the information at once, become frustrated, and eventually give up. A much better approach to applying the material is this: Take one point you wish to implement and practice this exclusively—both in your training session as well as in the rest of your life—for forty-eight hours and for at least two training sessions. Give this information priority over everything else. In this way, you will better understand the concept, remember it, integrate it with other knowledge, and effectively apply it in subsequent workouts.

Research from the field of educational psychology has shown that it takes up to twenty-one exposures or practices of new knowledge before it becomes ingrained, automatic, and "natural." It takes that long for new concepts to integrate into the existing body of knowledge. Just as in school or work, learning something new in your bodybuilding means that you have to practice it repeatedly until it becomes second nature to you.

Some of the information I will present may not be new to you, or it may be new words for some old common-sense wisdoms. That's okay. Translate these concepts into your own frame of reference. Practice these old concepts as well. It takes up to four exposures of old knowledge before it is effectively remembered and refined.

Just as we need plenty of repetitions in our physical training to teach specific muscles how to respond effectively to an exercise, we also need plenty of reps in our mental training to teach the mind how to work effectively with the body. Passively reading something once or twice is not enough. What you need to do is single out and repeatedly practice one point until you really know it. This is true learning.

If you follow these procedures in learning the system of mental training in bodybuilding, you will be amazed at how quickly you will master the information. It also can be a lot of fun. The mind was designed to work in conjunction with the body. When they work together, they provide more total energy than the sum of them working separately. This is the purpose of the book: to learn how to better use your mind with your body, so you can unleash a greater amount of energy into your bodybuilding. This is the Mind Pump.

1
Introduction

*B*odybuilders are remarkable people. They stand out from the crowd. Sure, they distinguish themselves by their physical presence, but they also distinguish themselves by exuding the poise and confidence that is rare today. They seem to present a sense of control, not only of their bodies, but of the rest of their lives as well.

Bodybuilders are dedicated and persistent men and women who spend many long hours in the gym grinding out "one more set" in order to achieve the kind of bodies they want. From these long training sessions, most bodybuilders have learned to appreciate all the wonderful complexities of their bodies. They have learned not only how one muscle group works with another, but also how nutrition affects the muscles, what kind of recuperation is best, and how their bodybuilding can integrate with other fitness activities.

Their bodies are their laboratories. Here they experiment with different training approaches and techniques to discover what works best. However, their bodies are also their studios in which they mold themselves ever closer to their ideals. Like sculptors, bodybuilders continually form, chisel, and refine their bodies. Bodybuilding can really be seen as pure art . . . pure creativity.

However, bodybuilding is much more than fitness, science, or art. It is also a form of self-expression and even personal therapy. People immerse themselves in their own world of fitness, feeling, controlling, and extending individual muscle groups beyond what they thought was possible. From their conscientious training, many bodybuilders eventually realize that if they can control and develop their rhomboids, for example, they can also extend this sense of control and development into the rest of their lives. So pumping iron not only works out the stresses of the day, improves fitness, and develops the body, it also provides perspectives and confidence that can be applied in the rest of life.

Bodybuilding offers people many things. One important benefit successful bodybuilders have embraced is that in order to effectively develop their bodies, they have to effectively apply their minds.

The Link

Most coaches and sports psychologists agree that at advanced levels of all sports and physical activities the mind accounts for anywhere between 60 and 90 percent of successful performances. In such activities as competitive archery and shooting, rock climbing, and aikido, the mind approaches 100 percent responsibility for good performances. After the physical skills have been learned and integrated, it is the mind that is in charge of producing these skills in consistent and effective ways.

Even at novice and intermediate levels of all sports and physical activities, the mind can play a crucial role in accelerating learning, retention, and development. Unfortunately, most people at these levels are so preoccupied with just the physical aspects of the particular activity that they never learn how to rely on their minds. They tend to move mindlessly through the activity with little conscious awareness of what their bodies and minds need to do.

On the other hand, some activities are so complicated that people mistakenly believe they have to monitor and direct minute details of the action. These people really do not trust their bodies and their previous training. They become exhausted trying to direct every little movement. The actions become disjointed or fragmented, and overall progress is slow and inconsistent.

Bodybuilding has one of the most direct mind-body links of any sport or activity. For better or for worse, *what goes on in the mind directly influences what goes on in the body*. One of the things that first attracted me to bodybuilding, some fourteen years ago, was this mind-body link. Sure, I loved the feeling of my muscles pumping and burning, but I also loved experiencing the direct control my mind could have over my body. I found that when I was mentally prepared for and involved in my training, I had fantastic workouts and made significant progress.

We've all had training sessions where our minds were so tuned in to our bodies that it almost seemed that our minds were *in* our muscles. We felt we could control every little movement and experienced the burn, pump, and even the individual muscle cells being stimulated. On the other hand, we've also had sessions where it seemed that our minds had absolutely no connection with our bodies. We could honestly not recall what muscle groups we worked. And then we wondered why we didn't get anything out of that workout!

These experiences show us that we can control the degree to which our minds link up with our bodies. We have the power to decide how and when to coordinate the efforts of our minds and bodies. Consciously choosing to do so is the same as choosing not to involve our minds with our bodies. Only we can make the choices of how to involve our minds in our bodybuilding.

The "More Is Always Better" Myth

Many of us grew up believing that doing more of everything will always produce better results. As we matured, many of us discovered that this principle was less and less valid. In our bodybuilding, we believed that if we mindlessly pumped out more and more sets we would achieve proportional results. However, what we usually experienced was just the opposite: By mindlessly pumping out more sets, we became overtrained. The more overtrained we became, the slower progress we made. "More is always better" is a myth.

Progressive bodybuilders are intelligent people who understand that mindlessly pumping out endless amounts of sets does not work and, in fact, is counterproductive. These people realize that when they use their minds to plan, program, and monitor their workouts, they achieve much greater results more quickly and with fewer chances for injury or overtraining.

Successful bodybuilders understand that in order to maximize their bodies, they must also maximize their minds. By the mind and body working together toward a common goal, the sum of their energies is actually greater than their individual efforts. This is called *synergy*. Combining the mind with the body in bodybuilding can produce results far beyond what mindlessly pumping out sets can do.

Mindful Bodybuilding

Purposefully applying the mind to workouts is what I call mindful bodybuilding. This approach is not metaphysical or mystical, nor does it require a doctorate in psychology to understand and apply it. Simply put, mindful bodybuilding is a common-sense approach that employs an easily applied system to maximize workout gains. Basically, mindful bodybuilding uses the complete mind to help shape a complete body.

Where there is a great temptation to space out from oneself during a workout, mindful bodybuilders have achieved significant results in really tuning into their bodies. They have found that they can more directly control the muscles being worked. They have also found that the results they attained not only were more effective, but took less time as well.

Mindful bodybuilding accentuates the direct mind-body link of weight training. It's a purposeful and systematic approach to maximize each workout, each set, and every rep. Mindful bodybuilding is also an effective way of unleashing more of one's overall potential. This approach may initially require more energy than mindless bodybuilding, but the overall control, progress, and development pay dividends many times over.

The Great Bio-Computer

The mind can be viewed as a great biological computer for the body. The mind as bio-computer is a useful metaphor for directing the mind into concrete bodybuilding progress.

Those of you who have any knowledge of computers know that *what* and *how* you put something into the system determines what and how the system will perform for you. In other words, the quality of the input determines the quality of the output.

The same can be said for utilizing the great bio-computers of our minds in our training. It is not only important what we program into our minds with our thoughts and attitudes, but it is also important how we do this programming as well. This mental programming tells us specifically what our bodies must do during a particular exercise. It creates a kind of kinesthetic blueprint—a mental sensation—of how our desired results will look and feel. Our minds thus provide us with the plans, direction, and even the energy to achieve the kinds of bodies we want.

Our minds are crucial to our bodybuilding success. Programming and using the mind properly allows us to tap into a great reservoir

of energy that we can let loose into our training. The degree to which we actively use our minds in our training often makes the difference between reaching our goals and falling short of them.

Self-Assessment

Our minds are wonderful tools in our bodybuilding, but we have to learn how to use those tools appropriately. A necessary starting point in learning the psychology of bodybuilding is to assess how you currently employ your mind in your training.

Take a couple of minutes and fill out the following questionnaire. Check the item (or items) that best represents your attitudes or actions in the given situation. There are no right answers. *What is right is what is right for you.* However, by filling out this questionnaire you can discover some trends in your thinking as well as find out mental gaps that you need to address. If you choose two responses to a question, you may want to rank the responses to show which you give a higher priority. If none of the responses is appropriate for you, fill in one that best fits you in that situation.

1. I bodybuild to:
   a. look good.
   b. feel good.
   c. feel like I am accomplishing something.
   d. socialize.
   e. show off.
   f. meet my goals.
   g. other _____ .

2. I tend to focus more on:
   a. my better developed parts.
   b. my weaker parts.
   c. my overall proportions.
   d. what I need to do.
   e. nothing in particular.

3. I plan my training sessions:
   a. not at all.
   b. on the way to the gym.
   c. as I go along during the workout.
   d. a week in advance.
   e. over a week in advance.

4. During the workout I strive to:

   a. keep lifting more weight for more sets and reps.
   b. maintain the same level.
   c. plan when I will increase the weight.
   d. always vary the weights and intensity.

5. I usually work first:

   a. my strong body parts.
   b. my weak body parts.
   c. the same sequence I always do.
   d. whatever is convenient.

6. During a set I:

   a. count reps.
   b. generally space out until the set is done.
   c. focus on the weight being lifted.
   d. focus on proper form.
   e. feel the muscles being worked.

7. Near the end of a set when I am experiencing discomfort, I usually:

   a. give up.
   b. push harder.
   c. slow down.
   d. revel in it.
   e. go faster.

8. Between sets I usually:

   a. relax.
   b. talk to people.
   c. get a drink of water.
   d. stretch and flex.
   e. focus on the next set.
   f. do nothing in particular.

9. I use some kind of formal relaxation:

   a. never.
   b. before the workout.
   c. during the workout.
   d. at various times throughout the day.

10. I relax for my workouts by:
    a. doing nothing in particular.
    b. stretching.
    c. listening to music.
    d. closing my eyes and following my breathing.
    e. joking with friends.
    f. other _____ .

11. When I look at other people's bodies and development, I usually:
    a. feel intimidated.
    b. get depressed.
    c. give them credit.
    d. try to copy them.
    e. get inspired.
    f. don't look at anyone else during training.

12. When someone compliments my body, I:
    a. feel good.
    b. discount it.
    c. wonder what their real intentions are.
    d. train even harder.
    e. kiss my biceps!

13. I usually handle distractions by:
    a. ignoring them.
    b. telling someone to do something about it.
    c. doing something about it myself.
    d. becoming more distracted.
    e. cutting short the workout.

14. If my training partner doesn't show up, I usually:
    a. cancel or cut short my workout.
    b. train alone.
    c. find someone else that day.
    d. feel lost.
    e. focus on exercises or equipment I usually don't do.

15. If I cancel a workout, I usually:
    a. feel guilty.
    b. tend to cancel more of them during the next couple of weeks.
    c. never cancel workouts.

    d. feel okay about it because that's what I chose to do.
    e. let everything else in my life slide.

16. For me, socializing in the gym:
    a. is really why I go.
    b. has no place in serious training.
    c. is fine as long as it doesn't disrupt my training.

17. To me, *intensity* means:
    a. getting angry.
    b. trying really hard.
    c. bearing down.
    d. being like a wild animal.
    e. I don't use that word.

18. During the actual exercise, what percentage of the time do I associate (tune into my body) versus disassociate (space out)?
    a. 100/0 percent
    b. 75/25 percent
    c. 50/50 percent
    d. 25/75 percent
    e. 0/100 percent

19. For me:
    a. the weights always win.
    b. I always have to beat the weights.
    c. the weights are allies.
    d. I never gave it any thought.

20. For me, bodybuilding is:
    a. my life . . . I would be completely lost without it.
    b. nice, but I can do without it.
    c. something I have to do to stay in shape.
    d. the symbolic glue that holds the rest of my life together.
    e. a way to meet people.
    f. a place to show off and feel good.
    g. other _____ .

Now that you have completed the self-assessment, go back and see how the trends or patterns in your answers show the ways you mentally approach your training. Do you have no pattern in particular? Do you tend to space out? Do you play it by ear? Do you plan appropriately? Do you superanalyze? Do you like to socialize? Do you tend to be a tunnel-visioned animal?

Although there are no objectively right answers, successful bodybuilders do have in common certain ways they approach their training that you might need to adopt. This book will share these commonalities so you can develop your own unique mental approach to your training.

Challenges

I would like to leave you with two challenges to ponder before you read on. First, more bodybuilders are learning everyday how to better direct their minds in order to make their workouts more effective and efficient. After eight years of working as a sports psychologist with bodybuilders at all levels, I can now conclude that if you are not applying the mental principles presented in this book, you are falling behind, both in maximizing your own development and in keeping up with your peers who consistently use these principles.

The second challenge is this: If during your training you are not actively doing something *for* your body with your mind, I pose to you that you are really doing something *against* your body. There is no neutral ground when it comes to the psychology of body-

building. Like muscles, your thoughts and attitudes do not stand still. They are either progressing or regressing. You are either doing something constructive and productive for yourself or something destructive and counterproductive for yourself. It is as simple as that.

The choice is yours. Which do you choose?

Personal Applications

This book is not only meant to be read. It is meant to be *used*. To facilitate this, exercises will be provided at the end of every chapter to help you summarize and assess what you found to be important. I urge you to take the time to go through this section. By doing so, you will gain an edge in really remembering and applying the material in the chapter. Do it!

Mindful bodybuilding is a systematic process that actively coordinates the mind with the body in order to achieve significant and consistent training results. It is a tuning in of the mind to the body so you can maximize each workout, each set, and even each rep. In this chapter you were introduced to the importance of linking the mind with the body, and you assessed how you typically use your mind in your training. These are the first two steps in developing your system of mindful bodybuilding.

Answer "yes" or "no" to each of the following questions:

- What goes on in my mind has no effect on what goes on in my body. **yes   no**
- I usually let my mind wander during my workouts. **yes   no**
- What comes into my mind comes into my mind. I have no control over my thoughts. **yes   no**
- Putting in more sets will ensure good progress. **yes   no**
- I'm not an intellectual, so I shouldn't try to learn anything about using my mind in my training. **yes   no**
- There is no organized way of using my mind in my training. **yes   no**

If you answered "yes" to any of the above questions, you missed the following concepts:

- What goes on in the mind has a direct impact on what goes on—or does not go on—in the body.

- You can consciously choose to involve your mind in your workouts.
- More is not always better.
- There is an organized program available to apply the mind systematically and effectively in bodybuilding.
- You don't have to have a PhD to understand and use this system. All you have to possess are honesty and the willingness to learn about the psychology of bodybuilding.

The main points I learned—or was reminded of—from this chapter were:

1. _____ .

2. _____ .

3. _____ .

4. _____ .

What is the one point I will give priority to in practicing during the next forty-eight hours (list the days here: _____

_____)

in my workouts? _____

_____ .

2
Concentration

T he cornerstone of the psychology of bodybuilding is concentration. Any advanced bodybuilder will confirm that the mind can release tremendous powers into the body. This mental strength is not a matter of intelligence, but a matter of concentration. It makes sense that in order to get 100 percent out of your workouts, you have to apply 100 percent of all your energies. This means using your mind as well as your muscles.

As important as concentration is, many bodybuilders spend inordinate amounts of time and energy avoiding concentrating. Some will do almost anything to keep their minds off the workout. They blast music, make frequent trips to the water fountain, take five-minute breaks between sets, watch others, talk about bodybuilding, or simply space out. Others become overly aggressive and angry, like raging bulls in heat, thinking this will help them concentrate. These same people wonder why they cannot sustain their intensity.

Effective concentration means being able to tune in as well as sustain one's mental efforts. But just what is concentration and what are the components in concentrating well? This chapter will present a system to help you better understand and apply concentration. Some of the components we will explore include: the proper uses of intensity, optimal training zones, focusing attention and awareness, and controlling movements. Let's start by determining just what is this thing called concentration.

Defining Concentration

Concentration is frequently referred to in very general and vague ways and means quite different things to different people. The best way to start getting a handle on your concentration is to define just what it means to you.

Take a moment and list the major components, qualities, emphases, and other things you need to do in order to concentrate well during a workout: _____

_____

_____

_____ .

This might have been a difficult task for some of you because a lot of us have never taken the time to analyze the mental processes involved in our training. However, in order to achieve consistent gains, it is essential that you know specifically how you concentrate. Those who mentally go into never-never land during a workout are really setting themselves up for future disappointments and frustrations, for they never realize when they are stifling their efforts.

Concentration is a narrowing and sharpening of your mental focus so you can maximize your physical movements. It is your mind directing, monitoring, and making adjustments for your body so it can effectively stimulate the desired muscle groups. Effective concentration involves both a tapping into and a channeling of mental energies toward the task at hand, namely, doing the next set or rep.

Now, many bodybuilders and other athletes mistakenly believe that concentration is the mind leading and manipulating the body. Nothing is further from the truth. Concentration literally means ''a coming together to a mutual center.'' Effective concentration means bringing the mind and body together so that they can work in harmony with each other to produce significant results.

Personality Types

The ways a person can accomplish this coming together to a mutual center vary with the personality of the individual. For some, yelling helps stimulate and energize them. For others, quietly relaxing and going deep within themselves is the best way to concentrate. These are the two extremes. For most of us, effective concentration involves using each of these approaches at various times during a training session. The real trick is to learn when to employ each.

The type of personality we have determines how well we will be able to concentrate. I have found two basic types of bodybuilding personalities evident in the gym: the tryer and the doer.

The tryer continually finds new ways to give up. While frequently well intentioned, this person allows fears, doubts, discomfort, self-imposed limitations, and distractions to sabotage his or her efforts. Tryers may say they want to go all-out, but they covertly hold themselves back from really putting out. These people say to themselves, "Well, I'll try to make it through this set . . . but I don't think I can," or "I'm trying so hard to get a burn, but I just can't do it."

Perfectionists are a classic subgroup of tryers. Perfectionists spend so much time and energy trying to meet some unattainable standard of perfection that they never accept who they are or what they do.

All tryers misplace their concentration away from the task at hand so they really end up working against themselves. Disappointment

and discouragement lead to new fears and put-downs. All of this quickly becomes a vicious cycle so that tryers never seem to possess any resolve or accomplish anything.

On the other hand, doers set specific goals for the upcoming workout or individual set and make plans for reaching them. These goals help them jump-start the concentration. Whether focusing on the muscles being worked or on the path of the barbell, a doer zeroes in on the specific task at hand. Doers commit themselves and throw all their energies into the next rep.

The doer always finds a way to accomplish a predetermined task. The doer may concentrate differently at various points during a workout. For example, many doers find that it's useful to focus quietly on themselves early in the workout or at the beginning of an exercise. During these times they emphasize proper form and rhythm. Near the end of a set, at the end of supersets, or during a maximum lift, doers need to become really fierce. They know that this approach summons up more energy to get them through the ordeal.

The difference between these two types of people is clear: The tryer tries to do something while the doer simply does it. Now, this distinction may seem simplistic, but it is valid. Doing is simple, direct, and clear. And so is effective concentration.

The prerequisite for concentrating better is that you have to be a doer. If you spend all your time and energy during your workouts trying, you will be merely spinning your wheels. Do whatever you are doing. Even if it is at a minimal level of success, effectiveness, or efficiency, at least you are doing it. And then next set, do it better. Do it, and do it again.

Effective concentration is really an easy process. All that it involves is *directing your mental energies to a specific goal*. In order to do this well, you will need to unlearn and then relearn the proper uses of the single most misunderstood component of concentration: intensity.

The Problems With Intensity

Intensity is the most overused concept today in all of sport. Athletes, coaches, and fitness writers just love using this term. They all advance the fallacy that learning to become more intense is the secret for success.

Sure, we must become intense during our workouts, but we have to learn how to channel our mental energies appropriately. For many bodybuilders, mental intensity is the feeling they wish to attain before a set. For them, being intense assures them that their minds are locked into the task at hand. However, too often people mistakenly equate intensity with trying harder. The problem with trying harder is that this usually takes you out of your most efficient and effective zones of functioning.

Many of us grew up with the notion that when things were not going well, all we had to do was to try harder and we could force things to go better. The problem with this logic is that the usual reason why things were not going well in the first place was because *we were trying too hard already*. And trying even harder simply took us further off course.

The problem with becoming more intense by trying harder is that we try to summon more energy and strength from unrelated outside sources. In bodybuilding, these outside sources are usually other muscle groups that should have no roles in assisting the muscles being worked. For example, if I am trying really hard to churn out a couple more barbell curls, I might try to enlist other muscle groups such as my lower lats or even my abs to get the bar up. So I swing the bar up, lean backwards, and shrug my shoulders to get the bar up. After a while, the only thing this accomplishes is that it actually pits one muscle group against another. Then I am working against myself and setting myself up for an injury.

The key to the proper use of intensity is not to try harder, but to try smarter. The wonderful comedienne Lily Tomlin has a profound line that goes, "Ever wonder why no one ever tries softer?" This may initially seem crazy, but in most cases when you ease off trying so hard, things go more smoothly and effectively.

Think back to some recent situation at work or school when things were not going well. It seemed that everything you tried to overcome the problem just made it worse. If you got angry, frustrated, or tried harder, it simply had the opposite effect of what you wanted.

At some point during this process you might have thrown up your hands and taken a break. Then the solution came to you precisely when you were not trying to find it! By easing off, slowing down, and trying softer, you found the solution. Things seemed to fall into place.

During a maximal bench press attempt, for example, the times when you repeatedly try hard to force the barbell up are usually met with failure. If you keep trying harder, it seems that you do not even get close to pressing the bar. Conversely, the times you stay within yourself and effectively channel your energy are met with greater success. Trying softer is more effective than mindlessly trying harder.

Now, I am not saying that bearing down is useless. Bearing down while staying within yourself produces better results than trying too hard and working against yourself. Bearing down while staying within yourself is the essence of intensity.

Igniting Your Training

True intensity means finding energy and strength *in* you (literally, "in-tension") and channeling it out in a focused manner. I like to use the analogy of a magnifying glass in the sun to convey the correct use of intensity. When most of us were kids, we used to start fires with only the aid of a magnifying glass. We discovered that the magnifying glass intensified the existing rays of the sun. As we aligned the magnifying glass to the proper angle, the sun's rays became so intense that they ignited a piece of paper.

Our concentration is our magnifying glass of mental intensity. We need to keep our concentration focused on the task at hand so we can ignite our training. Those who use the trying-harder approach to intensity really have no mental magnifying glass. Their approach is to try and find five more suns to start the fire!

In our workouts we need to focus our concentration so that our mental energy is like sand going through the neck of an hourglass. Stay within yourself, coordinate your efforts, and intensely focus on the next rep. This usually means to focus on the specific muscles being worked throughout the full range of motion. Become so tunnel-visioned with tuning in to your muscles that you are aware of nothing else until you are done with the set and your muscles are begging for mercy!

The proper use of intensity is to channel your existing energies in a focused way to the exercise you are doing. Like water going through a hydroelectric dam, focusing our mental energies in a concentrated way actually increases the power of our training. Our workouts become a high-voltage experience!

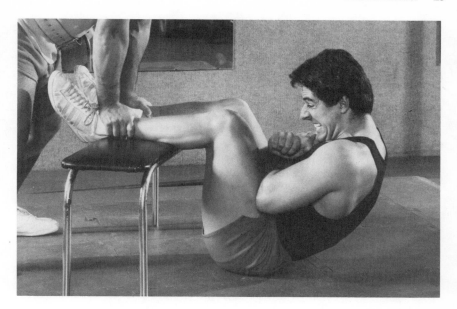

Optimal Training Zones

In bodybuilding as well as in the rest of our everyday activities, we have what I call an optimal zone of functioning. Once in this zone, we can attain effective results with a minimal amount of stress and strain. The optimal training zone provides the base for consistent bodybuilding gains.

Achieving an optimal training zone requires less effort than many believe. An example is in order. Today's cars are designed and engineered so that their optimal zone of functioning is around fifty to fifty-five miles per hour. In this zone the car achieves good results (speed) with efficiency (good gas mileage) and little wear and tear on the parts. Sure, I can "push the pedal to the metal" and go ninety miles per hour. This is called a maximal level of functioning. At this speed I achieve better results (getting somewhere quicker), but with less fuel economy, more wear-and-tear on the parts, and an increased chance of having an accident or seeing those little red revolving lights in my rearview mirror!

In our bodybuilding we want to have enough intensity to achieve an optimal level of functioning. In this zone, we attain results by allowing our muscles to work together and recuperate fully. We need a sufficient amount of intensity to bring us up into this zone.

If we fail to do this, we are not getting much out of our training and are really just going through the motions.

Once we are in this optimal zone of training, we need to use just enough intensity so that we can remain in this zone. If we apply too much intensity, we will cross over a fine line that pushes us beyond this optimal zone so that we really work against ourselves. The trick to training intensity is to find out where your fine lines are and to stay just short of them.

This optimal zone of training intensity is summarized by the diagram in Figure 2.1.

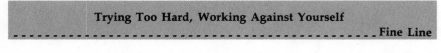

Figure 2.1.   Optimal zone of training intensity.

Now, I do not want to give the impression that this optimal zone of training intensity is not demanding. Quite often this zone is very demanding and might approach 90 percent of a maximum effort. Once in this zone, you can effectively and safely stimulate your muscles and give them a chance to strengthen. As your muscles strengthen over the course of weeks and months, you can progressively elevate this optimal zone higher and higher. This is the format of intelligent training.

Staying in your optimal training zone also helps you endure long workouts. It makes sense that the more efficient you are in your energy expenditures, the longer you can sustain your efforts. Bodybuilders who exceed their optimal training zones by being too intense and trying too hard waste precious energy, so they have little of it at the end of the workout. Appropriate intensity means both focusing in as well as sustaining quality efforts.

Granted, there are times when you may want to push yourself beyond your optimal zone and give a maximum effort. However, it must be understood that your success in these maximal lifts depends on developing the strength, technique, and resiliency from consistent training in optimal zones of functioning. A maximal effort also implies that you will have to take some time out to recuperate and go back into your optimal zone so that you can build again.

Maximal efforts are challenging and exhilarating indicators of progress that cap off weeks of hard training. However, do not lose sight of the fact that maximal efforts are based on a series of consistent optimal efforts. Achieving these optimal zones of training provides you with the strength and balance to attempt maximal efforts.

Zooming Your Concentration

Like our muscles, our concentration has various ranges of motion. Versatile and enduring concentration is dependent on being able to zoom in and out. At one end of the concentration spectrum is the narrow, pinpoint focus called *attention*. At the other end of the spectrum is the broad and expansive form of concentration called *awareness*. Attention is more of an active process that expends energy in a directed way (for example, "paying attention"), while awareness is more of a receptive process that provides perspective and endurance (for example, "becoming aware").

Both attention and awareness are crucial in concentration during our workouts. We need to pay attention to the specific muscles being worked in order to achieve the best stimulation. However, we must also be aware of how one muscle group relates to another so we can achieve the balance and proportion we desire.

At various times during our training we need to emphasize each form of concentration. For example, during a set I want to pay very specific attention to the muscles I am working so I can stay appropriately intense, giving optimal stimulation with minimal risk of injury. During warm-ups, breaks, evaluating myself, and posing, I would want to be aware of the interplay between muscle groups to learn how they influence one another so I can improve my overall symmetry.

We can liken attention and awareness to a telephoto lens on a camera. Sometimes we need to zoom in to pick up specific details while other times we need to zoom out in order to take in the big picture. In the same way, we can zoom our concentration in and out to make it more adaptable, appropriate, enduring, and complete.

Control

In bodybuilding, control is the name of the game. I am sure we have all seen novices or show-offs in the gym who quickly bang the weights down with a crash, thinking that they are getting a good workout. During the bench press, for example, they strain to get the weight up and then drop the bar back down on their chests. The result is that instead of getting big pecs they get bruised ones and sometimes even fractured sternums.

These "hot dogs" do not understand that a muscle can be fully stimulated only by a series of controlled movements. Controlling the muscle effectively means that you have to concentrate exclusively on that particular muscle. How can you control the weight or your muscles if you do not control your thinking? Effective concentration implies that you have to be in control.

Some advanced bodybuilders take this notion of *control* a couple of steps further so that they strive to tune in so fully with the muscles being worked that their consciousness is actually *in* those muscles! These bodybuilders actually get to the point where they identify so strongly with the muscles being worked that their identity is that muscle. This is the hallmark of bodybuilding concentration.

Psychologists have a fancy name for this process. They call it *locus of control*. This essentially means that *only you can influence you*. You are the captain of your metaphorical bodybuilding ship and only you can chart the course to your development.

Locus of control implies that no one can make you mad, distracted, frustrated, jealous, or even intense. You make yourself that way. Or you can allow someone—or something—else to do it to you. In either case, at some level of your consciousness, you are deciding to allow other people or other things to influence you.

I do not have control of everything in the gym. I do not have control of the person blaring his ghetto blaster, the woman who is using the machine I want to use, some idiot repeatedly banging the weights down, or other such distractions. However, *I do have complete control* of how I react to those distractions. I can allow myself to get all wrapped up in them, or I can tune in to the next set I need to perform.

Now, all of us become distracted at times. The important thing is to get back on course as quickly as possible. In this way, you can maximize what you can control, namely, your exercises and your muscles.

On one hand, effective concentration is really tuning in to yourself to focus your mental and physical energies in an intense way. On the other hand, effective concentration is staying in charge of yourself and controlling what you can control.

If you can actively assert control over such little things as muscle fibers, these little things will eventually become big things!

The System of Concentrating

Okay, you now know more about concentration than you ever did before (or, perhaps, ever wanted to know!). The next step is effectively applying these concepts.

First, you must convince yourself of the necessity of concentrating during a workout. Sure, it takes a little more energy to concentrate as opposed to spacing out, becoming constantly distracted, or mindlessly going through the motions, but the results you achieve will be well worth it.

In order to help convince yourself of the necessity of concentration, ask yourself, ''What do I go to the gym to do?'' If your answer is something like, "to have fun" or "to socialize," fine, but don't expect to achieve steady gains. If your answer is, "to train," good, but realize that in order to maximize your time and energy at the gym, you have to concentrate on what you are there to do.

It is helpful to plan your workouts ahead of time and prepare to apply yourself intensely. As you are driving to the gym, changing, or stretching, start narrowing down your attention to what you want to accomplish. And then go about doing it.

Realize that your workouts will rarely go as planned and there will always be distractions. Get back on course as quickly as possible. By keeping your mind on the tasks at hand, you will soon find that you are getting better workouts in less time. You will achieve a more complete pump or burn in a concentrated hour-long workout than you ever did in a three-hour mindless session.

At first, concentrating for long periods of time may be difficult. Take heart in the fact that the more you exercise your concentration, the stronger and more sustained it will become, just like your muscles.

Continually focus your mental camera and zoom in (pay attention to specific muscle groups) or zoom out (become aware of the interrelationships between muscles and overall balance). Use your mental magnifying glass to focus your mental and physical energies so intensely that your muscles will sizzle! Your workouts will then be more concentrated.

Review the key points below, which are essential to effective concentration. Put a check by the points you understand and put a star by those points you have to get a better handle on and practice.

1. Remember that concentration is a narrowing of your mental focus.
2. Always be a doer instead of a tryer.
3. Have specific plans for each training session. For example, plan for the specific muscle groups you want to work, the sequence of exercises you want to do, and specific techniques (supersets or negative reps, for instance) you want to use.
4. Channel your intensity as you would direct the sun's rays through a magnifying glass.
5. Stay within yourself.

_____   6. Learn what an optimal training zone is for you and stay within it. This is the only way to remain as intense near the end of your workout as you were in the beginning.

_____   7. Learn how to effectively zoom your concentration in and out between attention and awareness.

_____   8. Focus only on what you can control, specifically, your muscles and the next rep.

_____   9. Keep in mind that properly practicing your concentration will strengthen it, both in intensity as well as endurance.

The main points I learned—or was reminded of—from this chapter were:

1. _____ .

2. _____ .

3. _____ .

4. _____ .

What is the one point I will give priority to in practicing during the next forty-eight hours (list the days here: _____

_____)

in my workouts? _____

_____ .

3
Developing the Blueprint for Growth

Concentration implies having something to concentrate about. This "something" is our bodybuilding goals. At any level, establishing goals and making specific plans to reach those goals are *the* essential keys for bodybuilding success. These goals provide us with the game plans or the blueprints, if you will, for consistent progress.

Setting goals is crucial. How do you know what to focus on, what to persist in, or what to be inspired about, if you don't have goals? Creating clear and detailed bodybuilding goals gives you an idea—and even a vision—of the body you would like to achieve.

Now, there are still some bodybuilders around today who believe that goal setting and planning are a waste of time, so they hit the iron and go through set after set of mindless pumping. They tend to put in very inconsistent efforts. One workout is tremendous while the next is lackluster. There is also little continuity and progression between sessions for these people. Then these same people complain and wonder why they are always injured or lack motivation. They may also discover that they are grossly disproportioned (for example, all torso and no legs or all front and no back).

I have worked with many bodybuilders who are apprehensive about using goals in their training. Many of them fear that if they establish goals and don't achieve them, they must then consider themselves failures. Some others feel that they would be rigidly and mindlessly bound to any goals they set. Still others believe that it is just plain too much work to set up bodybuilding goals.

People who are apprehensive about goals do not understand the power of goal setting. Establishing goals provides us with the sense of purpose, direction, and even the initial impetus to achieve them. When I have clearly defined bodybuilding goals, I become eager to start striving for them. For example, when I have given a priority to improving my abs, the goal of washboard-like abs is fixed in my mind. Every sit-up, crunch, and leg lift I do is then tied into that goal. It seems that little else matters until I have reached my goal.

Having goals also provides me with a framework for expending my energies efficiently. Once I have specific goals in my training, everything I do can be measured against those goals. By setting goals, I can better stay on course during a workout.

You see, we are goal-oriented creatures. We need to have direction and to strive toward things. All of us naturally utilize and even rely on goals in our everyday living. We set goals for what we want or have to accomplish, which errands to run first, how to spend our time, and even how we wish to present ourselves to others. Without goals we could not get out of bed in the morning!

Regularly setting goals in our training is not a waste of time. On the contrary, setting up goals is an investment in our time. Establishing bodybuilding goals is really a natural extension of how we utilize goals in the rest of our lives. With clear-cut goals we can be much more proficient in our training than if we aimlessly wander

from one unrelated exercise to the next. Defining and working toward specific training goals are *the* quickest ways not only to employ your mind, but to improve the quality of your training as well.

My goal for this chapter is to present to you the system for using goals in your bodybuilding. As you use goals, you will not become a mindless robot. By regularly establishing and utilizing goals, you will discover more personal power that you can unleash in your workout.

Let's start with exploring just exactly what you want.

Goal Assessment

Goal setting and planning are really not that difficult. All they require is a little time and a lot of honesty. Take some time right now and write down here your bodybuilding goals for the next two months. Go ahead and do it!

To _____

To _____

To _____

To _____

Now, look at what you wrote. If you used such phrases as, "to be big all over," "to keep on pumping the way I have been," or "to build twenty-four inch arms," that is a good start, but you need to be a little more specific. Quite often, our goals are much too vague and general. Still, writing these general goals is far better than not writing down anything because you believe you do not need to do that or you believe you already know all your bodybuilding goals.

Any goal setting and planning must begin with an honest assessment of where you are now. Look in the mirror or have pictures taken of you and study them. Develop the kind of objective eye that discriminates size, proportion, and symmetry. Without judging yourself, honestly assess what is good and what is below par. Just accept what you find. Deluding or harshly judging yourself will serve only to retard and discourage you. This first self-assessment provides the solid base upon which you can establish your goals and devise your plans.

Bodybuilding Dreams

Goal setting is systematic, but I do not want to give you the impression that it is unemotional. Many of our incentives toward bodybuilding come from our dreams and aspirations. I think it is important to recognize and integrate our dreams and aspirations into our goals. These emotions become the fuel that fires our determination.

Go ahead, let your mind wander now and dream about the kind of body you would like to sculpt out. Write down that description here:

_____

_____

_____

_____

You might find it helpful to include body parts from bodybuilders you admire. We often need models to define for us what we would like to possess. For example, if you are a male bodybuilder, you might aspire to have the arms of a Sergio Oliva, the chest of an Arnold Schwarzenegger, the delts of an Albert Beckles, the back of a Franco Columbo, the sheer mass of a Lee Haney, the abs of a Richard Gaspari, the legs of a Tom Platz, and the symmetry of a Frank Zane. How about that for a body! Or, if you are a female bodybuilder, you might aspire to have the arms of a Kay Baxter, the chest and abs of a Corrina Everson, the delts of a Mary Roberts, the back of a Carla Dunlap, the legs of a Clare Furr, and the symmetry of a Diana Dennis all rolled into one!

Our dreams and aspirations are hazy, emotional images of what we want to become. In order to properly use them, we need to transform them into specific goals. One way to begin is to answer the following questions:

"How would you feel being stronger and more developed?"

_____

"How long and often would you have to train to attain this?"

_____

"What would you have to sacrifice?"

_____

"What would you have to learn or refine?"

_____

"What would you have to do to improve your lifestyle?"

_____

"And how badly do you want to do it?"

_____

Answering general questions like these provides you with the perspective you need to transform your dreams and aspirations into more concrete goals.

Assessing Individual Factors

Okay, let us get a little more specific in assessing your bodybuilding goals. Below is a list of some factors you may want to consider. Check those factors you really want to improve, write down the specific goal for improving that factor, and write down a number from 1-5 to indicate how important this is for you to improve (1 being low priority, 3 being a moderate priority, and 5 being a top priority).

Check		Factor	Specific Goal	Rating
	Size:			
5	44 3/4	Chest	48"	
4	53"	Shoulders	55"	
5	46'	Back	49"	
3	16½"	Arms	17"	
5	39½	Abdominals	36"	
3	25½	Thighs	27"	
3	15¾	Calves	16½	
	Proportion:			
5		Chest to Back		
4		Shoulders to Chest		
3		Chest to Arms		
3		Thighs to Calves		
5		Torso to Legs		(cont.)
5 ✗		BACK to WAIST		

Check	Factor	Specific Goal	Rating
	Symmetry:		
_____	Left Arm to Right Arm		
_____	Biceps to Triceps		
_____	Left Pec to Right Pec		
_____	Left Deltoids to Right Deltoids		
_____	Left Lat to Right Lat		
_____	Abdominal Symmetry		
_____	Left Thigh to Right Thigh		
_____	Quads to Hamstrings		
_____	Left Calf to Right Calf		

Now look at what you assessed. How discriminating were you? If you checked nearly every factor and rated it a 5, the assessment probably was not too helpful. But if you filled this chart in thoughtfully, you can begin to identify and prioritize body parts that need the most attention.

Occasionally review all these assessments. They are helpful in retaining the perspectives of what you want your body to become.

Doing these kinds of assessments may initially seem tedious, but they are essential in devising a blueprint for your bodybuilding success. In a way, these assessments are the metaphorical paper on which the specific blueprints are drawn. Now you are ready to start drawing.

Specificity

The cornerstone of any goal-setting system is specificity. Vague and general goal statements like "to have a big chest," "to feel good," or "to become more massive," won't cut it. You need specific goals that are concrete, observable, and measurable.

The parameters in devising specific bodybuilding goals are what I call the "Twin A's": The goals must be *appropriate* and they must be *attainable*.

The appropriateness of goals keeps them realistic. "I want 23-inch arms by next Wednesday" is not appropriate. When you structure goals on an all-or-nothing basis, the result is usually nothing. Structure your goals to be appropriate to what you have done in the past, where you are now, and what you deem feasible to do in the future. Say something like this: ''Given the time I have available to spend training, increasing my arms by a half-inch during the next nine months is feasible.''

When you construct goals that are appropriate, they become more attainable. Each little goal may not be too significant in itself, but because it has been reached, it provides the momentum to continue on to the next goal. In this way, your goals become progressive and you stay more motivated and dedicated.

The establishment of appropriate and attainable goals is like a ladder. The appropriateness of the goals is the frame of the ladder that is parallel and structured. The attainableness of the goals is represented by rungs that are spaced close enough to allow a smooth and steady climb.

For example, if I wanted to increase the size of my arms by an inch during the next nine months, my goal ladder might look like the one shown in Figure 3.1.

Each of these subgoals is fairly easy to attain in itself and flows together so that I can climb up the ladder to reach my ultimate goal

TO INCREASE MY ARMS BY ONE INCH

To barbell curl 150 lbs. in a maximal lift

To develop a dumbbell curl/kickback ratio of 3:2

To be able to do concentration curls for four sets of ten reps with 80 lbs.

To be able to do tricep kickbacks regularly for four sets of twelve reps using 30 lbs.

To bring my smaller arm's biceps up to par with my larger arm's biceps

To do forced or negative reps twice a week

Measure my arms in 4 1/2 months

To be able to do four sets of triceps pressdowns for four sets of twelve reps with 50 lbs.

To be able to do five sets of up-and-down barbell curls going up to 100 lbs.

To be able to do four sets of pullovers with 80 lbs.

To get a good pump in my biceps and burn in my triceps from each workout

To build a good foundation of strength in both arms

Measure my arms now

Figure 3.1. Goal ladder.

for my arms. Specifying training goals gives me the blueprint and the power to achieve the kind of results I want.

Prioritizing

Establishing goals implies that some of them are more important or relevant than others. This means that we have to continually prioritize our goals in order to keep them appropriate and attainable.

Successful bodybuilders always keep in mind what their training priorities are. It is so easy to get off track in the gym. Distractions abound for those who do not stay focused on their training priorities.

The secret of succeeding with priorities is this: There is quite a difference between setting a goal and *living with it*. These are two separate processes. Many struggling bodybuilders I know mistakenly assume that just because they establish a plan it will automatically come to reality.

On the contrary. Establishing a goal, committing yourself to that goal, and giving it a priority are just the beginning steps in bringing it to reality. You must live with the implications and demands of that goal. It is one thing to say you are giving a priority to improving your triceps, for example. It is quite a different thing to give them a continual priority in your workouts.

This is where the Muscle Priority Principle (see Appendix) has been valuable. Too many bodybuilders work the parts of their bodies early in a workout that are the most developed and of which they are most proud. These people usually put off working their weaker parts until later in the session. When it comes time to work these weaker parts, they usually do not have the energy or concentration to really exercise these lagging parts. The Muscle Priority Principle essentially says to practice what you preach in your goal setting. If you have given a priority to building your lagging triceps, then work them early in the training session when you are still fresh and eager.

Living with your priorities means learning how to say "no" to anyone or anything that might take you off course. There will always be temptations, options, and distractions during every workout. You must learn to say "no" to them. By saying "no" what you are really saying is "yes" to your priorities.

Prioritizing your bodybuilding goals and living with these priorities keep you more focused during your workouts, so you can more consistently maximize your time and accelerate your progress.

Long-Term Planning

Establishing specific goals is essential for maximizing individual workouts, but goals can also be applied in longer time frames in order to promote more complete and balanced development. There are three approaches to control your long-term planning: time lines, training cycles, and training logs. Let's look at each in greater detail.

Time Lines

Time lines are simple and effective tools that help you organize and plan the sequence of your training needed to attain some important long-term goal. This goal may be to win a contest nine months away or to look good on the beach this summer. Time lines help you manage all the details of your training so you can attend to the things that need to be addressed.

Time lines can be seen as training maps that plot out the sequence of events and desired dates of achievement. They detail the specific subgoals in the order that has the best possibilities of leading to the ultimate goal. Using our ladder example from earlier in this chapter, a sample time line would look like the one in Figure 3.2.

Now you develop your own time line. Think of some long-term bodybuilding goal you have. This goal should be comprehensive enough to encompass your overall development. Record this goal along with its completion date by the star on the time line in Figure 3.3. Next, plot out all the specific subgoals, sequences, and desired achievement dates along this time line. You will see in the figure below that some subgoal lines are longer than others. This is because they are more essential than others. For example, building up lagging hamstrings is more important than getting a tan. You will also notice that some subgoals are grouped closer together than others. This is because these subgoals necessarily blend into one another.

Now, go ahead and fill in the time line in Figure 3.3, and plot out your plan for a major long-term bodybuilding goal.

As you organize your time line, include not only the skills and experiences you wish to attain, but also the attitudes you wish to emphasize. You may also want to include logistical considerations as well, such as travel plans, tape recording, or posing suit fittings.

As you go through the process of attaining your subgoals, frequently refer to your time line. Feel free to modify it by adding, deleting, or combining subgoals or by changing the sequences and

Date		Subgoal
1/1		Measure arms
2/1		Build a good foundation
2/5		Obtain a good pump and burn from every workout
3/1		Do five sets of pullovers with 80 lbs.
4/1		Do up-and-down barbell curls with 100 lbs.
5/1		Do five sets of tricep presses with 50 lbs.
5/15		Measure arms
6/1		Do forced or negative reps twice a week
7/1		Bring up to par small arm's biceps
7/15		Do five sets tricep kickbacks with 35 lbs.
7/25		Do four sets concentration curls with 80 lbs.
8/1		Develop a 3:2 ratio between dumb-bell curl and kickback
8/15		Do a good set of barbell curls with 150 lbs.
9/1		INCREASE ARMS BY ONE INCH

Figure 3.2.   Sample time line.

completion dates. By staying flexible, you will be able to keep your time line relevant and useful.

A time line gives you observable and concrete feedback on your

Date   Subgoal

_____   _____   _____

_____   _____   _____

_____   _____   _____

_____   _____   _____

_____   _____   _____

_____   _____   _____

_____   _____   _____

_____   _____   _____

_____   _____   _____

_____   _____   _____

_____   _____   _____

_____   _____   _____

_____   _____   _____

                    Major Goal: _____*

Figure 3.3.   Time line.

progress. Sometimes we become so immersed working on specific things that we lose sight of where we are going. A time line helps us retain the perspectives of the big picture.

Some bodybuilders combine three or four time lines into a yearly plan. These are called training cycles.

Training Cycles

Successful bodybuilders understand that they continually have to alter the emphasis of their workouts in order to achieve balanced development. For example, at some time during the year they may want to work on basic strength exercises. At other times they may want to strive for maximal lifts. Still, at other times they may want to work on complementary muscle groups (for example, triceps and biceps or hamstrings and quadriceps). Finally, they may want to work on their symmetry and getting cut.

Expanding time lines into yearly training cycles helps better organize and sequentialize long-term training. Top bodybuilders plan, at the most, three or four training cycles a year. A couple of these training cycles may culminate in a peak such as a competition or an important event in which they want to look good. Each cycle may emphasize different body parts, types of routines, training intensities, various advanced techniques (such as superset or stripping), nutrition, and other related fitness activities (such as aerobics, powerlifting, HeavyHands, or learning a new sport). As you can see, with so many variables to attend to, one has to be organized. Plotting out such training cycles provides this organization and gives the bodybuilder a greater sense of control over his or her time.

Here is the sequence of some of the major points from the training cycle of a competitive bodybuilder with whom I have worked.

- Build basic strength through:
  —Bench press —Squats —Deadlifts —Pull-ups —Barbell curl
- Use more pyramiding
- Go for some maximal lifts in bench press, squat, and barbell curl
- Decrease poundages, but increase reps and sets
- Start working on some specific muscle groups, especially triceps, posterior deltoids, hamstrings, and lower abs
- Regularly utilize supersets, forced reps, and some negative reps
- Develop contest time line

— Look at contest date and get registration in
— Assess proportion and symmetry
— Work on deltoid balance
— Start to revise posing routine
— Do some regular bicycling, rowing, or aerobics three times per week
— Give higher priority to back training
— Cut down on calorie intake
— Work more on tan
— Practice posing one hour a day
— Be really positive and eager
— Get ripped!
— Travel
— Do the very best at the competition
— Come home and recuperate with light training and fun activities for three weeks
— Plan out new training cycle

Generally, training cycles progress as follows:

— Basic exercises > Specific exercises
— Heavy weights with low repetitions > Lighter weights with high repetitions
— Isolated muscle groups > Related muscle groups
— Working on deficiencies > Working on overall proportion
— Mass > Symmetry
— Quantity > Quality

Make sure that in each training cycle you include time for rest and recuperation. Just as recuperation from each workout provides the time for the exercised muscles to recover and strengthen, recuperation from a training cycle provides the time for the mind and body to rejuvenate and recharge. During these times, you may want to participate in other sports or activities, experiment with new types of training machines, or even stay away from the gym entirely for a while. Do not fall into the trap of placing guilt trips on yourself such as, ''I should be training now,'' or ''All my hard work is melting away.'' Both your body and your mind need breaks in order to heal and refresh. Give yourself these breaks so you can start the next training cycle healthy and eager to attack the iron!

Regularly utilizing training cycles is an intelligent way to organize and monitor long-term progress. As you can see, training cycles can become pretty detailed. It is crucial to plan accurately and chart your whole cycle. All of this implies that you need to keep a training log.

Training Logs

You may feel overwhelmed by all of the components of effective goal setting. Trying to remember your time lines or where you are in your training cycle can become extremely confusing. This is why I am a great believer in maintaining a training log.

Training logs help in six general ways.

1. Training logs relieve us of the burden of having to remember all the specific details of our training.
2. If we are on some kind of two-day split, double split, or fourteen-day training cycle, our logs can help us stay organized and on track. This, then, will free us to concentrate on the training session.
3. Training logs serve as wonderful comparison standards that help us monitor our training. Bodybuilders who maintain logs for years have a detailed history of their improvements.
4. Training logs provide us with concrete feedback that indicates how we are progressing in accordance with our goals. They give us perspective on the big picture.
5. These records can provide us with clues for slow progress. Muscle gains are rarely linear (that is, proceeding along an expected line at the same rate) so continually monitoring yourself with the aid of a training log will keep you in a position to make the necessary adjustments in your training.
6. The physical act of writing in a training log facilitates commitment, dedication, and concentration. It seems that the more I write, the more I stay tuned in to my training.
   Here is an example of the entries a top woman bodybuilder made in her training log for a one-week period.

Monday: a.m. workout: chest, shoulders, and abs
                          pyramid bench press—five sets, incline flies—four sets, dips—three sets, upright rows—five sets, laterals—four sets, bent laterals—four sets, crunches—two sets, sit-ups—two sets, hanging crunches—two sets.

              p.m. workout: taught two aerobic classes

Tuesday: p.m. workout: back, triceps, and legs
                            superset lat pulldowns with cable
                            rows—four sets, dumbbell rows—
                            five sets, hyperextensions—two
                            sets, tricep extensions—four sets,
                            tricep pressdowns—four sets,
                            kickbacks—four sets, pyramid leg
                            press—four sets, squats—four sets,
                            leg extensions—three sets, leg
                            curls—three sets

Wednesday: a.m. workout: rowing machine for forty minutes

              p.m. workout: taught two aerobic classes

Thursday: a.m. workout: chest, biceps, and abs
                            incline bench press—five sets, in-
                            cline flies—five sets, pyramid bench
                            press—four sets, pyramid barbell
                            curl—five sets, dumbbell curls—
                            four sets, up-and-down concentra-
                            tion curls—seven sets, easy curls
                            (with negative reps)—four sets, sit-
                            ups—two sets, wall crunches—two
                            sets

              p.m. workout: shoulders and back
                            military press—four sets, upright
                            rows—four sets, laterals—four sets,
                            pull-ups—two sets, bent barbell
                            row—four sets, hyperextensions—
                            two sets, lat pulldowns—five sets

Friday: a.m. workout: triceps, legs, and abs
                            pullovers—five sets, superset tricep
                            pressdowns and kickbacks—four
                            sets, pyramid hack squats—five
                            sets, leg extensions—three sets, leg
                            curls—three sets, seated calf
                            raises—six sets

              p.m. workout: taught extra aerobic class

Saturday: p.m. workout: chest, shoulders
                            up-and-down bench press—seven
                            sets, incline bench press—four sets,

flies—four sets, dips—two sets, stripped military press—four sets, upright rows—four sets, pyramid laterals—five sets, bent laterals (with forced reps last two sets)—five sets

Sunday: p.m. workout: went for two-hour bicycle ride

You can see that this woman varies her workouts tremendously, emphasizing different combinations of muscle groups in every training session. She says by doing so, her muscles are always forced to adapt. She also says that she would be lost without her training log. She keeps extremely detailed records on not only her workouts, but her physical and mental reactions as well. Her records give her an indication of what muscle groups need to be worked—and in which way—in the next workout.

You would be amazed at how many top bodybuilders have kept meticulous training records. Frank Zane has kept a detailed log for many years. He knows that in order to really maximize every training session, he has to know what specifically he has to do. He says that when he is having trouble with a particular muscle group, he goes back to his records from years ago when he was also having trouble with the same muscles. He usually finds answers to his problems in his old logs.

Training logs are an example that, besides being dedicated athletes, bodybuilders are also intelligent personal scientists who systematically chart and monitor their progress. Armed with this information, they are in good positions to make steady, consistent, and progressive bodybuilding gains.

"Ready, Fire, Aim"

I do not want to leave you with the impression that you should be so structured and formalized in your planning that you become like a robot, mechanically going from one prescribed exercise to the next. Our plans are blueprints, nothing more. They are meant to be used, modified, refined, and used again.

Goals imply action. George Morrisey, one of the pioneers behind the management-by-objectives movement in business, said something about goal setting that can be applied to bodybuilding as well. He said, "The purpose of goals is not to produce goals. The purpose of goals is to produce results." Once we have our bodybuilding blueprints in the form of specific goals, time lines, and training cycles, we have to do something with them. Start out by following your planned routine, but always feel free to make the kinds of adjustments that will keep your goals appropriate and attainable.

This approach of implementing your goals in your workouts is best summarized by the "ready, fire, aim" philosophy. Unlike the classic "ready, aim, fire" approach, "ready, fire, aim" emphasizes action. It is through this process of doing that we gain the experience and knowledge we need to revise our goals and make them more useful.

After they have discovered the powers of goal setting, some bodybuilders mistakenly believe they should have perfect goals before they do anything. So they spend their time elaborately defining their goals, but do very little with them. The effective use of goal setting requires implementing them. It is through this process of *defining, doing,* and *refining* that you can keep your goals appropriate and attainable.

As you train, make sure to continually monitor and assess your progress. This will give you the feedback necessary to make the right adjustments as well as give you incentives to continue. Don't be afraid to look in the mirror. This is not a pathological form of narcissism, but merely an information-seeking procedure. You may also occasionally want to have photos taken of you from different angles. Get as much feedback as you can, so you will be able to plan your future bodybuilding goals.

As you proceed, do not hesitate to alter or change your goals altogether. Goal setting implies constantly making new goals. Follow your goals as long as they remain appropriate. Do not feel bound to inappropriate goals just because you think you should follow them. For example, if you have planned to make some maximal lifts in the bench press, do not feel bound to attempt them just because your time line says you should. Do not let your goals use you. Use your goals.

Plan, prioritize, adapt, modify, but *do* something with your goals. Fire now, aim later.

The Goal-Setting System

Goals are essential to consistent bodybuilding growth and development. They provide the structure and the blueprint from which you can proceed. They also provide the initial impetus to achieve your goals. In this sense, your bodybuilding goals and plans are a springboard from which you can create the best possible you.

The following is a checklist of the key components of goal setting and planning. Put a check by those points you understand and put a star by those points you need to better learn and practice.

_____ • I have goals for each workout as well as for two weeks and six months from now.
_____ • Having bodybuilding goals gives me the structure and framework so that I can have a purpose in my training.
_____ • I use my bodybuilding dreams to formulate my goals.
_____ • My goals are always appropriate and attainable.
_____ • Establishing goals and living with them are two separate processes. I must give priority to implementing my most important bodybuilding goals.
_____ • I have a written time line charted out for at least the next two months.
_____ • I understand the concept of training cycles, especially how they culminate in a peak and how they must also include recuperation time.
_____ • I regularly use a training log to chart and plan my progress.

_____✓_____   • I understand that goals are empty without applying
them. I use the "ready, fire, aim" approach to effectively implement and refine my goals.

Apply your goals and plans to every workout. Have a clear picture
in your mind of what you want to accomplish before you enter the
gym. Tom Platz always visualizes what he wants to do as well as
how he wants to feel before every training session. If you wait until
you get into the gym to determine what you want to do, the odds
are that it is already too late. Your mind and body need time to
integrate your plans, so determine your plans well in advance.
Whether at home or work or driving to the gym, use this time to
clarify your plans.

At the beginning of this chapter, I asked you to write down your
bodybuilding goals. Now that you are armed with all this additional information about goal setting, I would like you to answer
the same question: "What are my bodybuilding goals?"

For the next workout? _____Be There, Focussed_____
_____and Intense_____

For the next week? _____Continue Tonda on staying_____
_____

What are my specific plans to reach these weekly goals?
_____Get to the gym, rest, eat right_____

For the next month? (Use a time line if you wish.) _____Cut out_____
_____Sugar, project do at work 40 wk_____

What are my specific plans to reach these monthly goals?

_____

For the next training cycle? _____
_____At least 10 lbs_____

What are my specific plans to reach these training cycle goals?

_____

Remember, it is fine to have nicely worded goals in your training
log, but these goals imply doing something with them. Goals without action are like a barbell without a bodybuilder: The structure
is there, but there is no use for it.

The main points I learned—or was reminded of—from this chapter were:

1. _____ .

2. _____ .

3. _____ .

4. _____ .

What is the one point I will apply or practice during the next forty-eight hours (list the days here: _____

_____)

during my workouts? _____

_____ .

There is a classic maxim that goes, "If you do not know where you are going, you will almost surely end up somewhere else." There is also a corollary to this that goes, "If you do not know where you are going, any route will take you there." The choice is yours: You can do nothing and flounder, or you can plot out your body-building course and eventually succeed. If you know where you are going, and how to get there, the chances are you will.

How to maintain and even increase the energy in achieving your goals is the subject of the next chapter.

4
Staying Motivated

I n all the speeches, seminars, and workshops I give to athletes and business people, there is one question that I get asked more often than any other. And that is, "How can I get more motivated?" By the way, this question is usually asked by a person with a weak and whimpering voice!

Motivation is a very popular topic in bodybuilding. However, like the weather, people like to talk about motivation, but very few seem to know what to do about it. Most bodybuilders seem to talk about it only when they don't have it. Motivation in bodybuilding, as well in the rest of life, seems to be a very elusive entity.

Much of the confusion about motivation revolves around the fact that people refer to it in very general, vague, and even mystical ways. "If I only had more motivation, then I could blast my pecs"; "I need a good dose of motivation for my workout today"; "C'mon, Kubistant, motivate me"; and "I wish I had the motivation of Albert Beckles" are examples of how vague motivation can be. If you asked these people just what they meant by motivation, they would probably shrug their puny delts! These people mistakenly believe that there must be some kind of magic pill, recipe, or gimmick that will immediately make them more energized, dedicated, and intense bodybuilders.

There is no magic pill. Being motivated in every training session is essential for staying focused, intense, and on track. This chapter will help you better understand motivation and apply it in your workouts.

Becoming Versus Staying Motivated

The first step in better understanding motivation is to realize that there is an important distinction between becoming motivated and *staying* motivated. Becoming motivated is really pretty easy. I become motivated when I see someone really putting out in the gym, when I pick up a bodybuilding book or magazine, after I have had a couple of outstanding workouts, or when I receive compliments on how good I look. All of these sources inspire me to greater efforts.

However, the really challenging thing is learning how to stay motivated in my training, especially when those nice positive outside stimuli are not around. Staying motivated is a major key in putting in consistent workouts. Staying motivated is less influenced by situational occurrences such as receiving compliments or reading a magazine. It has its base in one's attitudes, beliefs, and goals.

So the critical issue of motivation is learning how to stay up for every workout. There is nothing magical about it. Staying motivated is a learned habit that takes a little awareness and effort, but pays dividends in providing consistent and regular results.

In order to better understand how to stay motivated in your training, take a little time now and answer this question: ''What kinds

of things do I need to regularly do, be, or have, in order to stay
motivated in my bodybuilding?'' _____

_____

_____

_____ .

Some of you may have responded with such answers as good
equipment, a regular training partner, previous successful workouts, appropriate and attainable goals, good nutrition, intense
concentration, or persistence. If you look at the types of answers
you gave, you will notice that they usually fall into two general
categories: those sources outside of you and those inside of you.

The Two Forms of Motivation

Successful bodybuilders understand that there are two forms of
motivation: *extrinsic* (external) and *intrinsic* (internal). Each form
is necessary in order to achieve consistent bodybuilding gains, but
as in cooking, one has to know when to use each ingredient.

Extrinsic motivation comes from sources outside us. We become
inspired when we view a bodybuilding competition, receive compliments and support from friends, or read and learn about new training approaches. Once we become motivated in this way, we then
usually seek to copy, repeat, and continue to apply these inspira-
tions. The challenge with using extrinsic motivation is that unless
we integrate it into our belief systems and lifestyles, we will soon
run out of the willpower to continue.

You see, willpower (or self-discipline) is a very finite entity. For
example, right now as you are reading this, see how long you can
stay angry. Go ahead . . . be angry! For most of you, the longest
you could stay angry was about two minutes. What usually happens is that your resolve diminishes, you become distracted, and
then return to reading this. Arnold Schwarzenegger has said that
discipline is necessary only in doing something that you do not
want to do! Unless the sources of our extrinsic motivation are connected, are integrated with something more personal and meaningful, our willpower will not be strong enough alone to sustain our
energy.

Extrinsic motivation is nice. It is the frosting on the cake. However, this implies that there has to be a cake in the first place. And this metaphorical cake is called intrinsic motivation.

Intrinsic motivation is that energy that emanates from our inner goals, desires, needs, and wants. Although it is not as flashy and overtly emotional as extrinsic motivation, our intrinsic motivation is the energy that keeps us focused, striving, and persistent.

Intrinsic motivation comes from what is meaningful to us. The key to understanding this form of motivation is to break down the word itself. Ask yourself this question: "What are my *motives* in my bodybuilding?" Since there will probably be many layers of answers to this question, take your time in answering it as completely as you can.

1. _____
2. _____
3. _____
4. _____

You may want to return to this question when you finish reading this chapter or at some later date in order to gain a broader perspective on your bodybuilding motives. Answering it completely is important.

As you discover some answers, you will soon see how one relates to another. Once you find out your motives in your training, you will then be better able to understand how they influence your bodybuilding goals, needs, wants, desires, drives, dreams, and aspirations.

Establishing the connections between your motives and your goals and desires is important because each feeds the other. For example, when I am really psyched for an upcoming workout, I am more likely to establish appropriate and attainable goals. On the other side of the coin, when I have the structure for my training provided by my goals, I am more likely to be excited about reaching them. Motivation and goal setting must be continually linked so that they can build upon each other to provide more concentrated training.

The more specific you become in describing your bodybuilding motives, the more sense they will make to you because you have connected them with other things that are important to you. Once you have done this, your motivations will become more concrete and manageable so you can more easily channel them into your

training. The net result will be that as you operate on these more specific and tangible levels, you will stay more motivated in your training.

Attitude Power

One quality common among bodybuilders who stay motivated in their training is that they have a realistic and pervasive positive mental attitude (PMA). These people have discovered the powers of PMA and have not only integrated it into their training, but the rest of their lives as well.

A strong positive mental attitude is grounded on the following realization: In any situation we face or any decision we make, we can approach it only in one of two ways—in a positive, optimistic, and building-up point of view or a negative, pessimistic, and tearing-down point of view. There are no other choices. There is no middle ground. I also submit to you that *if you do not know how you are approaching a situation, you are really dragging yourself down.*

But how come more of us do not actively choose to be positive more often? You see, it takes much more awareness, courage, creativity, dedication, and just plain guts to be positive. Becoming pessimistic is simple. It just requires doing nothing actively for yourself. Then your fears, doubts, and insecurities will creep in and drag you down into being negative.

This notion of essential choices is really quite simple. In today's hectic pace of life with so many changes, options, and alternates, it is refreshing to discover that I can approach these situations in only one of two ways. And since I have just explained these two choices, only a fool or a masochist would choose to be negative. So I really only have one choice and that is to be positive.

Being positive is an active process that involves conscious choices to build yourself up. Being positive is not wishing, hoping, or some kind of pie-in-the-sky attitude. Rather, it is a realistic affirming of yourself and what you choose to do right now.

Being positive is really a matter of perspective. A few years ago, the Peace Corps had a television commercial that showed only a half glass of water. The announcer then asked, "Is this glass of water half full or half empty?" He went on to say that if you viewed it as half full, the people from the Peace Corps were interested in talking with you, because you were the kind of person with the attitudes they wanted. The same perspectives can be applied to bodybuilding.

Whatever perspective you choose is accompanied by a lot of power. Most bodybuilders are totally unaware of this fact. Whichever direction you choose, you set into motion the processes to achieve that particular choice. The power of our attitudes is best summarized by the famous radio commentator Earl Nightengale, who said, "You become what you think about." It is as simple— and profound—as that. You become what you think about. For better or for worse, for richer or for poorer, in sickness or in health, for stronger or for weaker, you become what you think about.

If you keep on focusing pessimistically on your puny pecs (for example, "My chest is just awful"), your pecs will remain small. Or, if you say, "There is no way in the world that I will be able to squat that amount," there will be no way you can.

On the other hand, if you say, "Look how far my lats have come and let's see just how much more I can improve them," chances are you will continue to improve them. Or if you say, "I am going to give my best shot at curling that weight," chances are you will.

In bodybuilding, as well as in the rest of our lives, what we accomplish is governed by the principle of the self-fulfilling prophecy. What we decide we can or cannot accomplish, we will probably actualize. I think this principle was best summarized by Mark Twain when he said, "If you think you can or if you think you cannot, you're probably right!"

We continually have to recognize and reinforce what we have, instead of what we have not. Sure, top bodybuilders search for deficiencies, but they always place them within the larger framework of improving themselves even further. They say, for example, "If I build up my lagging calves, I will become more balanced and proportional." The secret of PMA is that as you remain realistically positive and optimistic, you tap into a huge inner reservoir of energy that you can channel into your training.

Part of staying positive and motivated is working out and surrounding yourself with genuinely positive, dedicated, and supportive people. Motivation can be quickly clouded or even eroded by negative, sarcastic, inconsiderate, or deficiency-oriented people. Top bodybuilders continually reinforce themselves and associate with other positive people. They have learned that their bodybuilding progress has no place for excuses, lies, fears, or nonbelievers.

The real test of your PMA comes when you have to be around negative people. It is easy to be positive when you are around positive people, but the real challenge is being positive when others are trying—consciously or not—to drag you down with their negative mental energy. Being positive means being positive all the time.

The more you choose to be positive toward your workouts and your overall development, the more you will tap into the powers of believing in yourself. Just as negative mental energy and pessimism feed each other, so do PMA and belief feed each other. The choice is yours. There are no other options.

As you focus on your positiveness, belief, and strengths, you will be amazed at how eager you are for your workouts and how long this energy lasts. Being realistically positive may initially require more commitment, but it opens up new sources of energy that will intensify your concentration, desire, and hence your progress.

Also, the more positive you remain, the more often you will tap into such other related qualities as courage, persistence, purpose, and just plain joy. These are the qualities that will sustain you during the low times. As you immerse yourself into your positive reservoir, you will discover that each quality complements and actually strengthens the others. So the more positive you are, the more energized you will become. The more energized you are, the more courageous you will become. The more courageous you are, the more persistent you will become. The more persistent you are, the more purposeful you will become. The more purposeful you are, the more joyful you will become. The more joyful you are, the more positive you will become. And on and on and on.

Positiveness begets positiveness. Choosing to be positive is contagious not only to other sources within you, but to others as well. As you continually choose to be genuinely positive, you will be surprised at how your attitudes and beliefs flow together. A realistic positive mental attitude is what keeps you motivated.

The System of Staying Motivated

I am sure that all bodybuilders have heard and read about the necessity of being motivated, positive, and on your own side. But do you *really* believe these things? Either you do or you do not. If you do, how can you apply them into your training sessions?

First, as we discussed in the last chapter, constructing appropriate and attainable goals is essential. This gives you direction and purpose. Goal setting and staying motivated go hand-in-hand toward effective bodybuilding progress.

Second, continually search for external sources of motivation to inspire you. Books, magazines, role models, encouraging training partners, and gyms with positive environments all provide incentives to stay motivated in your training. View these sources as investments in yourself.

Third, always remember and reinforce your specific motives in your training. These motives may change as you progress or vary at different times in your training cycles, so continually reassess them. Understanding your bodybuilding motives gives you extra energy that you can use in sustaining your training intensity.

Fourth, actively choose to be positive. Remember, you have only two choices: to be positive or to be negative. Choose to build yourself, be realistically optimistic, and believe in yourself. Convince yourself that you can accomplish anything you set your mind to. You are not out there to sabotage yourself, are you? So actively be positive and believe in yourself.

Remember, you become what you think about. Being realistically positive sets into motion all the powers and processes needed to attain your training goals.

Finally, surround yourself with other positive bodybuilders and actively support each other. Let the gym rats, show-offs, and ego kings and queens do their own things. You do not have time or energy for these people. Find people who share the same positiveness and dedication as you. Develop the kind of support system where just seeing one of your friends in the gym makes you more inspired and focused. Actively encourage your friends. By doing so, you may find that you actually have more energy to devote to your own training.

Now, I have had many bodybuilders come to me and say, "Okay, I'll give this positiveness stuff a try. What do I have to do to start being positive?" My answer is simple: Just start being positive! Being positive has no prerequisites, no preparation. If you must, start by pretending to be positive; you will soon genuinely be positive. Actively choose to be—and remain—positive. Do it now!

However, it is one thing to be positive. It is quite another thing to exude it. Just because you believe in yourself does not ensure that this will extend into your workouts. Actively exude the feelings of positiveness and self-belief. Be eager for each training session. Do not just go through the motions. Attack each workout, each exercise, each set, and each rep. Be goal-directed, focused, and intense. By being eager to maximize each workout, you might surprise yourself at how much energy you have and the kinds of results you achieve. ATTACK IT!

Use the following checklist to assess how well you understand this chapter on motivation. Put a check by those points you understand and have integrated into yourself. Put a star by those points you need to work on and practice.

_____ • I alone determine my own levels of motivation.

_____ • I understand that there is a crucial difference between becoming motivated and staying motivated.

_____ • Extrinsic motivation is nice, but I know I can't rely on it.

_____ • My sources of intrinsic motivation relate to my bodybuilding goals, drives, and aspirations. I understand what my motives are and use them to build upon one another.

_____ • In any situation I encounter—inside or outside the gym—I actively choose to be realistically positive.

_____ • I become what I think about.

_____ • I understand the necessity of being around and supporting other positive people.

The main points I learned—or was reminded of—from this chapter were:

1. _____.

2. _____.

3. _____.

4. _____.

What is the one point I will apply or practice during the next forty-eight hours (list the days here: _____)

during my workouts? _____

_____.

In order to help you stay motivated, I have available for you a free laminated reminder card on "Eight Keys to Staying Motivated." All you have to do is send a stamped, self-addressed envelope to me at P.O. Box 13309, Reno, NV 89507-3309, and one will be on its way to you.

Do it now!

5

Relaxation

*I*t may seem strange that after such an energizing chapter on motivation and positive mental attitude I should now talk about relaxation. During our workouts, we are supposed to stay contracting, flexing, and even tense, right? Relaxation seems to be totally antithetical to what we need during a workout. So why do we need relaxation?

Learning how to relax is essential for consistent gains and injury-free workouts. This chapter will present the basic formats of relaxation and give you an opportunity to start developing your own style of relaxing. In doing so, you will be better able to handle the pressures, stay in control, and maximize your progress.

The Rationale for Relaxation

Relaxation is the foundation for efficient and effective workouts. The more relaxed I am, the better I can clear and focus my mind. All bodybuilders already have a great deal of awareness and control over their muscles. Relaxation simply heightens this awareness and control.

The benefits of employing relaxation before and during workouts are based on one simple physiological fact: *A relaxed muscle can contract with more force and for a longer period of time than a slightly tensed one.* Think about this for a moment. It makes sense that if you want to maximize the contraction and the subsequent deep stimulation of a muscle, it should start from a state of relaxation.

Go ahead right now and experiment with contracting your biceps, first from a totally relaxed state and then from a slightly tensed one. Let your arms hang loose at your side and take a couple of seconds to allow your biceps to relax. See if you can feel the inner fibers loosening. Now tense your biceps. Now, relax them again, but this time leave a little tension in the muscles. Tense your biceps once again. Notice the difference of the force of the contractions between each attempt. Chances are that you will feel much more power when you contract your biceps from a relaxed position than from a slightly tensed one. If you would keep up this alternating for a few minutes you would also discover that you could keep this going for a longer time if you continually started each contraction from a relaxed state.

Another physiological fact in support of relaxation is that, by definition, the more relaxed a muscle is, the more oxygenated it is. This increased oxygenation allows for more complete contractions as well as for more efficient flushing away of the toxic by-product (that is, lactic acid) from the exercising muscle. So a relaxed muscle is significantly more efficient, responsive, and enduring than a slightly tensed one.

On a psychological level, when I am more completely relaxed, I can assert more accurate control over a specific muscle throughout its full range of motion. From a base of relaxation, I can be more aware of my entire self, pay particular attention to a desired muscle group, and channel my energies effectively in controlling that muscle group throughout the exercise. Also, it seems that when I start from a base of relaxation, I can endure more discomfort for a longer period of time than when I am slightly tensed. So relaxation keeps me in charge of my workouts.

The reasons why bodybuilders should employ regular relaxation practices go on and on, but I am still amazed at how many people rush into the gym forsaking any kind of relaxing or stretching and immediately dive into pumping iron. When I ask them why they do this, I usually receive the kind of response that is summarized by, "Look, I know relaxing is good for me, but I rarely have the time to do it." These bodybuilders believe that relaxing before a workout is nice, but it is optional.

Relaxing before a workout is not a waste of time! On the contrary, relaxing at home, at work, or in the locker room before a workout is an *investment* in your bodybuilding. Those who take the time to relax seem to have their workouts better organized, can react and adapt to their body's feedback, can endure more intensity and duration of discomfort, and can more quickly recover and recuperate. In short, when you take the time to relax, your training efforts tend to become both more efficient and effective.

Types of Relaxation

I believe that part of the reluctance of bodybuilders to go through a relaxation sequence is grounded in their confusion of all the different forms and styles of relaxing available. Some also mistakenly believe that these forms have some kind of magical or mystical connotations that will deprive them of their self-control. Many bodybuilders tell me, "I would like to learn how to relax, but I don't want to become involved in some kind of hocus-pocus movement." Indeed, when faced with all the relaxation approaches around, some bodybuilders become even more tense and anxious!

It really does not matter all that much which forms of relaxation you use. You can adopt any formal approach such as progressive relaxation, autogenic training, transcendental meditation, classical hypnosis, self-hypnosis, biofeedback, centering, or various forms of prayer and yoga. You can even integrate relaxation into martial arts training or go through a series of different phases of relaxation. With my clients I currently use eleven different types of relaxation that are modified from the above-mentioned approaches. Or you can develop your own style of relaxing.

All of these approaches have two things in common: (a) They achieve about the same brain-wave state, and (b) at one point or another, they emphasize breathing.

First, these approaches differ in the pathways they follow to relaxation, but once there, they all achieve the same physiological effects. This means that no matter which approach you use, relaxation is relaxation. Various approaches can do different things, but they all rely on achieving relaxation as a base.

Second, it is a physiological fact that *you cannot breathe fully and slowly for a while and be physically tense at the same time*. Following your slow and rhythmic breathing seems to be a natural tranquilizer. (Notice the words I used in this last sentence. I did not use words like *change* or *force*, but the more passive and soothing words like *follow* and *slow*. This is important.)

The critical point in relaxing is to develop your own unique style and then regularly use it. Emphasize what works for you. Don't

worry if you are doing it right. Any way that relaxes you is the right way.

The process of relaxing shows you how to control yourself effectively. If you can control yourself enough to relax, then certainly you can control the exercising of individual muscle groups.

A Sample Relaxation Sequence

Now that you can see the benefits of relaxing in bodybuilding, just how do you do it? Here is a general sequence that many formalized styles of relaxing follow.

Most forms of relaxing usually begin by helping you become aware of all your senses, one by one, the last one being your overall body sensations. They then have you scan the length of your body (usually from head to toe) becoming more aware of both individual body parts as well as searching for sources of tension, tightness, fatigue, or pain. Next, they have you passively follow the path of your breathing and as you do so, feel how the other systems and parts of your body slow down and relax. Finally, they have you pleasantly drift for a while and then, from this base, begin to focus your mind on what you need to do. All of this usually takes between five and twelve minutes and even less as you become more proficient with your own style.

For those of you who want a more structured sequence of relaxing, I offer the following transcription. This was initially published in my first book, *Performing Your Best* (Life Enhancement Publications, 1986). If you do not have a regular relaxation exercise, start with this one. If you do have a regular format, pick and choose pieces of this one and integrate them into your own existing style.

You may wish to make a tape of this or have a friend read it to you. In either case, speak or have your friend speak with a soothing voice. Frequently pause during and after sentences. If you are unsure about the pace, remember that it is better to go too slow than too fast.

Find a place where you will not be disturbed for about 15 minutes. Close the door, take the phone off the hook, and tell the kids not to disturb you. Next, take off as much clothing as you feel comfortable with. Especially make sure to loosen any belts or garments that constrict your waist. Make sure you take out your contact lenses if your eyes become irritated when they are closed for over ten minutes. If you lie down, be sure to lie on your back since there is more supporting structure there. Whether you sit or lie down, make sure your arms and legs are uncrossed because crossing them minutely yet significantly restricts the blood flow to the lower parts of your body.

Now, here we go!

When you are ready to, close your eyes and become aware of your presence in this room. . . . (five-second pause). Now that your eyes are closed . . . (three-second pause), start tuning into some of your other senses, beginning with your sense of hearing. . . . Ask yourself what kinds of sounds you hear. Outside the room . . . inside the room . . . within yourself. . . . Recognize that during the course of this, some sounds may distract you or your mind may wander. If this occurs, fine. Just catch yourself, come back on course, and go on. All of us become distracted at times. And all of our minds wander at times. The important thing is to come back on course. . . .

Now, tune into your sense of smell and note any subtle odors or fragrances. . . . Now tune into your sense of taste and note anything you can taste. How much saliva is there? You may want to feel your taste buds more by rubbing your tongue against the roof of your mouth. . . .

Finally, tune into your general body sensations. . . . Note how relatively hot or cold the room is for you. What parts of your body are warmer or colder than other parts? . . . What parts of your body are in contact with the chair (or the floor or bed)? . . . You may even feel some air brushing against your cheeks or arms. . . .

As you tune into your body, you may want to adjust your position in order to become even more comfortable. Now look for any sources of tension, tightness, fatigue, or pain in your body. . . . When you find one, gently move it and let the tension go. . . . There is no need to keep it tight. . . . If you are unsure whether or not a place is tense, experiment with tensing and relaxing that spot in order to feel the difference when it is tensed. . . . and when it is relaxed. . . .

Good. . . .

Now, shift your attention to your breathing. Don't change it. . . . just passively observe it. . . . Follow the path your breath takes as it goes in your nose . . . down your throat . . . and out again. . . . Allow yourself to ride the crest of your breathing . . . (ten-second pause).

You might want to imagine that your breathing is like gentle little waves washing upon a shore. As you breathe in . . . the wave comes in . . . and as you breathe out . . . the wave leaves. . . . See this scene. . . . Feel it. . . . Each time you breathe out— each time the wave leaves—it seems to wash away more and more tension, tightness, and extraneous thoughts from you. . . . You might even feel this tension or tightness being gently washed away and leaving through your fingers or toes. . . .

Good . . . .Now allow your breathing to change so that it becomes very slow . . . very deep . . . and very complete. . . . Breathe just fast enough so you don't feel the need to gasp for air. . . . Slowly breathe so that it takes you three . . . four . . . even five seconds to inhale . . . and as much time to exhale. . . . Very slow . . . very deep . . . and very complete. . . .

As your breathing slows . . . feel some of your other systems slowing down as well. . . . Heart rate slowing . . . thinking slowing . . . blood pressure dropping . . . digestive system slowing. . . . So that all of you . . . is slowing down. . . .

You may already have started to feel yourself sinking into the chair (or couch or bed). . . . Now, with each relaxing exhalation . . . you can actually feel yourself sinking farther and farther into the chair. . . . Sinking farther and farther . . . into being relaxed. . . .

Just let yourself drift . . . and enjoy the feel of being more . . . and more . . . relaxed. . . . (pause ten seconds).

Good. . . . Now I am going to count backward from four to one . . . and when I reach one, you can open your eyes. . . .

Here we go. . . . Four, (gently raise your voice here) your awareness is coming back into this room . . . back to your senses. . . . Three, you are feeling very relaxed and refreshed. . . . As we reach two, start moving around a little. . . . Moving your head and your arms, shrugging your shoulders, and stretching like a cat. . . . And now take a couple of final deep breaths . . . and one. . . .

Stretch and look around. Notice the differences in the way you feel now compared with before you started. Most of you will feel more relaxed. There may be parts of you that still feel tense or tight. This is okay. It may take several more times through this exercise to allow these parts to relax. In some cases, it took years for those parts to become tight, so it makes sense that it might take a while to have them return to a more relaxed state.

How long did it seem, did it feel, that you had your eyes closed? For most of you it would have seemed significantly shorter or longer than the actual time. This is because through relaxation we tune more into our own internal clocks instead of outside objective time.

If you fell asleep, that's okay. This is probably what you needed to do. If you continue to fall asleep during this exercise, do it earlier in the day. Also, before you start the exercise, program yourself to stay awake. Most of all, don't worry about it.

Note how long the feelings of relaxation last. For most of us, these feelings last somewhere between fifteen minutes and three hours. As you learn how long you usually stay relaxed, you can then plan another sequence about when the feelings are wearing off.

Practice and refine your relaxing so you continually develop your own personal style. As you do, you will better feel the benefits and see how it can be effectively applied into your bodybuilding.

The System of Relaxing

Relaxing provides us with a strong cornerstone from which we can unleash a tremendous amount of intensity, energy, and stamina into our workouts. Relaxing is a skill, and, like any other skill, the

more you practice it, the more efficient and effective your relaxing will become. That is, you will learn how to relax more fully in a shorter period of time.

Guidelines

It is essential that you develop your own individual style of relaxing. In the beginning, when you are formulating your own style, it is okay to use audiotapes, but shift to your own internal sequence as soon as you can. Avoid becoming dependent on any external source for your relaxing. Don't get to the point where you say, ''I can't relax today because the batteries in my tape recorder are dead!'' Learn to rely on your own inner monologue to guide you.

Do your relaxing at least twice a day: once in the morning and once before your workout. Waiting to do your relaxing at the end of the day does little good, for then you are weary from the stresses of the day. As you develop your own individual style of relaxing, you will find that you can become completely relaxed in just a few minutes. You can even learn how to relax with your eyes open. (This is especially wonderful at work or at school!)

All of this implies that you give relaxing a priority in your life. If you say to yourself something like, ''Well, I'll relax when I find the time," we all know that you will never find the time. Make relaxing part of your daily, and workout, routines.

Here is another hint about prioritizing your relaxing. The times you feel you have the least amount of time to relax are precisely the times when you need it the most. When you are rushed and feel you do not have time for yourself, you are the least effective. Learn to be aware of these times and let them become a stimulus for you to relax and take care of yourself. You will find that when you do so, you will return to your activities more refreshed and more effective than if you kept plodding along.

As you develop your own style, you will see how effective and even pleasurable relaxing is. Not only does it physically relax you, but it also puts you into a frame of mind in which you can really concentrate on your training.

Relaxing Before Training

Going through a relaxation sequence prior to training can prepare you both mentally and physically for the workout. Relaxing is a nice transition period from the rest of the day to your training.

It is important to find a place and time to relax that works well for you. Some bodybuilders relax at their homes or offices just prior to leaving for the gym. Others relax on the way to the gym. Still others relax in the locker room while they are changing their clothes or stretching. Those who relax while stretching refer to it as their "mental stretching." Just as physical stretching warms up the muscles and tendons, mental stretching warms up the mind to prepare it for the challenges ahead. Wherever you relax, do it regularly so that it becomes a part of your preworkout routine.

As you relax before the workout, scan your body, becoming particularly aware of sources of tension or tightness. Allow these tight areas to melt away under the influences of relaxation. You may even have to physically warm up these areas more in order to safely prepare them for the rigors of the upcoming workout.

As you relax, become aware of your various muscle groups, especially those you plan to exercise. This awareness will allow you to stay more in touch with those muscles during the actual workout.

Near the end of your relaxation you may want to review your specific goals for that training session. What muscle groups do you want to work? And in what ways? What exercises and in which sequences do you want to proceed? When do you want to do pyramiding, forced reps, or other advanced techniques? Clarifying your goals as you relax helps etch them into your mind so that you can begin your workout with a purpose.

One of the worst things you can do is rush into a workout. Take the time to relax. It will physically and mentally ready you, so you can get the most out of a training session.

Relaxing During Training

An increasing number of knowledgeable bodybuilders are also doing various forms of relaxing during their workouts. They find when they do so, they are better able to sustain their concentration and endure longer periods of discomfort. Just like relaxing before a workout, relaxing during a workout should become a priority.

The rationale for relaxing during a training session is based on this physiological fact: It takes relatively longer for a muscle to relax than it does for it to contract, and this difference is multiplied with fatigue. Relaxing during a workout gives your mind and body the opportunity to adapt more quickly to the stresses you are placing on them. Relaxing during a workout also allows you to pace yourself better so that you can put in the same quality sets at the end of the session as you did in the beginning.

Remember that all effective forms of relaxing are based on your breathing. Before the next exercise follow your breathing to tune into yourself. When you are changing plates or spotting for your partner between your sets, focus on your breathing to center and prepare yourself for the next set. Between exercises when you are looking at yourself in the mirror, or going to the water fountain, check in with your breathing. It will indicate whether you are physically and mentally ready to proceed. Follow your breathing. It is the pathway to self-awareness.

Some bodybuilders with whom I have worked have developed little techniques for relaxing during a workout. Some shrug their shoulders, adjust their clothing or lifting belts, roll their heads, stretch, or flex. They use these movements as cues to relax and get back in touch with themselves and what they need to do next.

Rely on your relaxation. It is home base for both awareness and control. Relaxation is the foundation for maximizing your physical and mental energies. As you apply relaxing to your workouts, you will quickly discover just how indispensable it is to quality training. Like your lifting belt or training gloves, relaxation is something you shouldn't leave home without!

A Relaxation Checklist

Here is a little assessment that gives you an opportunity to review the important concepts of relaxation. Place a check beside those points you already do well in your relaxing. Place a star beside those points you need to better understand or practice.

_____   • I can feel the difference in my muscles when they are relaxed versus when they are slightly tensed.

_____   • I relax at least two times a day.

_____   • I have developed my own unique style of relaxing.

_____   • I regularly relax before a training session.

_____   • When I relax, I become more aware of myself, especially the muscles I plan to work.

_____   • During this time I also review my specific training goals for that session.

_____   • I make time to relax during my workouts.

_____   • I follow my breathing or use little gimmicks to keep me tuned in to what I need to do next.

_____   • Relaxing is becoming easier, more effective, and more pleasant for me.

The main points I learned—or was reminded of—from this chapter were:

1. _____ .

2. _____ .

3. _____ .

4. _____ .

What is the one point I will apply or practice during the next forty-eight hours (list the days here: _____

_____)

during my workouts? _____

_____ .

Relaxation is an investment in controlled and progressive body-building. It is a nice state to achieve in itself, but it also provides the foundation from which the more sophisticated mental training approaches of visualization and affirmation can be directed. These approaches are the subjects of the next two chapters.

6 |
Visualization

I n the last twenty-five years, the applications of mental imagery have expanded by leaps and bounds. In popular circles, visualization has evolved to become almost its own separate branch of psychology. Still, we are just scratching the surface of possible applications of mental imagery in our daily lives.

Accordingly, the single greatest advance over the last ten years in the psychology of bodybuilding has been in the number of people who regularly use some form of visualization in their training. Elite bodybuilders have always been far ahead of their counterparts from other sports in the ways they use visualization, but today an ever-increasing number of intermediate and novice bodybuilders are relying on visualization as well.

As we utilize and rely on visualization in our training, it is becoming both more varied and more sophisticated. However, visualization is still easy to learn and use. This chapter will explore the basics of visualization and help you easily apply it in maximizing your workouts.

We are visual creatures. Approximately 83 percent of all new information comes to us through our sense of sight, while 11 percent comes to us through our sense of hearing, and the remainder comes through our other senses. We rely on vision much more than most of us are aware.

On an internal level, about 70 percent of us use our ''inner vision'' in our thinking, planning, creating, problem solving, and evaluating. We imagine possibilities, outcomes, and our roles in these processes. With our inner vision we create a mental picture that helps us pursue solutions.

One only has to look at some of our everyday expressions to see (sorry!) just how much we rely on the metaphor of vision. ''Picture this,'' ''imagine that,'' ''envision success,'' ''see with the mind's eye,'' and ''daydream about tomorrow'' are just some of our more frequently used expressions. The language of pictures provides concrete connections between the mind and the body, as well as the mind and outside reality.

Our uses of mental imagery have become so automatic that few of us realize how much we really use it. Most of us visualize how we are going to look with a particular combination of clothes when we are choosing them in the morning. We also visualize how the living room might look before we rearrange the furniture. Most of us also visualize how a word looks when we are figuring out how to spell it. Finally, most of us visualize the routes we will take around town when running errands.

The scientific applications of mental imagery have also been expanding tremendously. Today we use various forms of mental imagery in healing and self-regulation, relaxation, learning and retention, creativity and problem solving, psychotherapy, strategic planning, and performance enhancement. In all these areas, mental imagery has become an integral component that facilitates both the depth and breadth of the effectiveness achieved.

There is really nothing magical or mystical about mental imagery. It is a concrete and easily applied approach in utilizing different

parts of the brain and maximizing its functioning. The applications of mental imagery are just about as wide and varied as the mind can imagine!

The Types of Mental Imagery

Although there are many specific applications of mental imagery, they all can be reduced to two general types: *disassociative* and *associative imagery*. Both types can be effectively used in bodybuilding. Let's look at each in more detail.

Disassociative Imagery

Disassociative mental imagery is a spacing out from what you are experiencing at the moment. For example, during a tough set, I may space out from the discomfort I am experiencing in my muscles to get through the last couple of reps. So during these times my mind is not in the gym, but in a sunbaked hidden cove in Mendocino! Or when I am relaxing before a grueling workout, I might disassociate for a while to relax myself even further. During these times, I am not in the gym, but floating in a desert hot springs with my muscles being bathed in soothing warm water!

You can use this type of imagery to literally disassociate yourself from the here and now. Disassociative imagery can serve as a kind of mental anesthesia that takes your mind off the events at hand. This imagery helps you endure the uncomfortable times so that you can later effectively tune in to yourself. This tuning in is called associative imagery.

Associative Imagery

Associative mental imagery is an amplification of what you are experiencing at the moment. It is directed, controlled, and even programmed images that fine-tune your actions or plans. Associative imagery can be used for such purposes as monitoring, regulating, healing, and channeling personal energies. The purpose of associative mental imagery is to better control all the minute actions that are occurring at the moment.

Associative mental imagery is better known as visualization. Visualization creatively magnifies control of the task at hand. Arnold Schwarzenegger's visualization of his biceps becoming mountain peaks that fill up the whole room is a well-known example of how visualization can be used in bodybuilding.

I often employ visualization in my own training. During my warm-ups before the actual workout, I might visualize breathing in and out *through* my tight deltoids. That's right, through my deltoids. I would visualize that my nostrils were actually *in* my delts. Each time I inhaled I would visualize breathing in fresh energy, and each time I exhaled I would visualize breathing out the stiffness. Near the end of the workout when I found myself fatiguing, I might visualize cool, rich, oxygenated blood pulsing through and bathing the muscles being worked. These applications are irrational, but because they are, they allow us to use all parts of our brains. They work!

Visualizing involves me more closely with my body and helps me safely and fully stimulate the muscles being worked. Training books and magazines are constantly telling us to focus on the muscle instead of the weight being lifted. Visualizing can aid in this if you picture the striations of the muscle and how it contracts. Beyond that, visualization can help you feel how the muscle is being stimulated, whether the pump or burn is achieved, and how the muscle grows. Visualization focuses and directs all of your mental senses more specifically to control the muscles being exercised.

Using Both Forms of Imagery

Both disassociative and associative mental imagery can effectively be employed in bodybuilding. The key is to keep in mind the best applications of each form. Remember, disassociative imagery is best used when you want to relax or temporarily take your mind off the situation at hand. Associative imagery is best used when you really want to tune in and control the specific actions.

Many bodybuilders have achieved some significant results by disassociating. They disassociate early in a set to conserve their energy and concentration. Other bodybuilders employ disassociating imagery to aid in reaching a deep state of relaxation. Then they can pace themselves through a long training session and can better endure the rigors at the end of the workout.

The important thing to remember when using disassociative imagery is that it must be your conscious choice to use it. You must have power over it. Unconsciously spacing out is not using disassociative imagery. Intelligent bodybuilders know when they need to disassociate, and they control that process.

One factor seems to differentiate elite athletes in all sports from the very good ones: Elite athletes continually monitor and regulate (that is, associate with) their bodies. When good or recreational athletes are more likely to space out from themselves, elite athletes tune in to their bodies, searching for signals of stimulation, fatigue, or pain. As they discover such signals, they are able to adapt their workouts more quickly, based on the feedback they are receiving. This process is the foundation of the Instinctive Training Principle (see Appendix) where bodybuilders design and alter their workouts to keep them appropriate to what their bodies can take.

To maximize muscle control and stimulation, creative bodybuilders utilize a variety of associative imagery approaches in their training. Most bodybuilders really tune in to their muscles late in a set by visualizing the muscle fibers being stimulated and exhausted. Some take this visualization a step further by amplifying the feeling of the burn or pump. They visualize a searing red burn or a bloated hard pump in order to promote the feelings they are experiencing. Still others visualize their muscles so intensely that they actually feel themselves go into and even *become* those muscles. Finally, a few bodybuilders visualize themselves becoming some sort of an animal (such as a bull, lion, bear, or combination of animals) that represents all their positive bodybuilding qualities. These applications of

visualization in bodybuilding are as varied and creative as your mind will allow.

So experiment and learn how and when to apply both disassociative and associative imagery. In a way, disassociative imagery provides a base for effectively applying associative imagery. Don't discount spacing out in a purposeful way. However, by tuning in with associative imagery, you can create more applications for visualization and thus extend yourself better in your training.

One specific form of visualization is the culmination of all work done on mental imagery. Once learned, it can help better organize, program, and direct your workouts. It is something that we will explore in detail. This form of visualization is called *mental rehearsal.*

Mental Rehearsal

Mental rehearsal is the leading edge of the application of mental imagery into sport. It can be used in anything from programming the next set to rehearsing a competition months away. As the name implies, mental rehearsal is a visualization approach that reminds, practices, refines, and even programs the mind and body specifically for the upcoming task.

Without being aware of it, we rely on mental rehearsal in our everyday lives. We mentally rehearse what we are going to say to a mate or boss, how we want to come across in a particular situation, or how we would like to perform during a test or speech. We can use these same processes in mentally preparing for our training sessions.

Research Support

The effectiveness of mental rehearsal—as well as any other form of mental imagery—is supported by the following scientific findings.

The first series of findings revolves around the neuromuscular responses from visualizing. From the classic research initially done by Edmund Jacobsen in the 1930s, it was found that *the basal parts of the brain and the central nervous system could not differentiate between something that was actually happening versus something that was being very vividly visualized.* The higher parts of the brain do this differentiating. So when I am mentally rehearsing my next set of leg extensions, all those nerves that stimulate my quads are firing minutely yet significantly. Hence, my body believes that I am actually pumping my quads, programs the proper action, and even gains experience in doing this exercise well. In this way, specific rehearsal provides an effective neuromuscular link so that what I visualize directly affects the desired muscles.

The second set of research findings centers on what Richard Magill and other motor learning theorists call the *cognitive link*. It seems that when I vividly visualize all the components of a complicated action, I am so cognitively involved that the mind-body connection becomes integrated. So, for example, when I am mentally rehearsing all the emphasis of a pullover (low hips, bent and wide elbows, flat back, spread chest, and contracting triceps, for instance), my mind and body are so locked into one another that motor commands are immediately understood and implemented.

The third set of findings is based on the current work by brain researcher Dr. Karl Pribram and the people at Sybervision. They suggest that *when you vividly visualize something with all your mental senses, you are actually physically creating the specific electromagnetic properties of that thing.* Simply put, this means that you are actually creating what you visualize!

Whenever you mentally rehearse something in vivid detail, you are also creating an electrical field of that thing. And as the quantum theory of modern physics tells us, whenever there is an electrical field present, a magnetic field also occurs. This magnetic field then attracts whatever is being mentally rehearsed. More than ever, hard science is proving to us that what we see is what we get!

Strange? Eerie? Metaphysical? Impossible? Think about this last proposition for a moment. We really do have more power and control over ourselves than we may be aware. Science is finally developing the research sophistication and technology to measure those phenomena that many of us have believed in and practiced for years. Sources ranging from grandmothers to teachers to holy books have historically preached that whatever you think, you will attract to you. Well, we are starting to prove that the brain can actually do this. By mentally rehearsing something in vivid detail, we are really creating the electromagnetic fields to bring this visualization into reality.

All of these research findings have many implications for bodybuilding. It's actually difficult to fully comprehend and appreciate what these findings are suggesting. In order to help you grasp and believe in the powers of mental imagery, I want you to think back to the times in your life—both inside and out of your training—that you have performed, achieved, or become the exact things you vividly dreamed about, visualized, or rehearsed. Stop for a moment now and recall those instances.

The bottom line with all of these research findings is that, properly programmed and rehearsed, our visualizations can accelerate the development of the kind of muscles we desire. We really do become what we think about.

The Components of Mental Rehearsal

Many iron heads often joke that they are mentally rehearsing a workout when they are going to take a nap. Mental rehearsal is no substitute for good, hard, and consistent training. However, many research studies have confirmed that combining mental rehearsal with the actual activity is much more effective than doing either separately. Mental rehearsal is a valuable supplement to the physical activity. If we can use the analogy of the body being a sophisticated computer, mental rehearsal is the programming function that directs the computer how best to perform.

One of the beauties of mental rehearsal is that you can employ it in almost all phases of your bodybuilding. You can mentally rehearse your next set, your next workout, or if you are competing, your performance in an upcoming contest. Tom Platz is a fervent believer in the powers of mental rehearsal. He mentally rehearses not only each upcoming workout before he leaves for the gym, but every detail of his performance at the next Mr. Olympia competition as well.

I like to use Denise McCluggage's (1977) conception of the components of mental rehearsal. She breaks down mental rehearsal into three specific components: *mental preplay, mental replay,* and *mental splicing*.

Mental preplay is the rehearsing of specific actions immediately before the action. Prior to a set, I mentally preplay not only the muscles I want to work, but also the specific feeling I want to achieve (such as a bloating pump or a searing burn). Mental preplay gives me the opportunity to prepare my workout as well as program my mind and body so they can effectively work together.

Once into the workout I might pause at various times and check whether what I am doing fits with my mental preplay. This process is called mental replay. As in replaying a videotape, mental replay gives me the chance to compare my goals to my execution. If there is a discrepancy, I can usually detect the differences.

Once I have discovered a discrepancy, I am then in a good position to change it. This process is called mental splicing. If the error lies in faulty programming, I would then visualize myself actually cutting out that counterproductive section of my mental preplay and splicing in the new desired rehearsal. If the error lies in my implementation, I would cut out what I was imprinting in my memory from my actions and then splice in the desired version. In either of these two ways, I am then "re-membering" my mental rehearsals.

These components of mental rehearsal can also be used following a workout. In the shower, when I am dressing, or as I am driving home, I might mentally replay the whole training session, reinforcing what I did well and searching for errors in my form, tempo, or concentration. I would then splice in the desired actions and mentally preplay the whole new workout approach again.

Mental preplay, mental replay, and mental splicing are complementary and cyclical processes. Each leads and depends on the other to form a complete mental rehearsal. By using these three components you can eventually develop a mental videotape that is the program for dynamite workouts.

Although I have been focusing on using these components in an individual workout, mental rehearsal can also be employed toward a contest or exhibition. Even if the performance is months

away, you can use mental rehearsal to program and reinforce how you want to look, your graceful and powerful posing, and your air of overall confidence. For example, I would mentally rehearse myself on the stage feeling huge and defined, the lights and cameras focusing on me, the crowd going wild, and my being in total control. Hence, even if I have never been on a particular stage before, by using mental rehearsal my mind and body gain valuable practice in performing well there.

The applications of mental rehearsal are becoming more expansive and widespread every year. Once learned, mental rehearsal is an essential tool for unleashing both the mind and body into every workout.

The System of Visualization

Using any form of mental imagery is really not all that complicated or difficult. We use our mind's eye continuously throughout the day. All visualization entails is that we direct these everyday processes into our workouts.

I do not want to give the impression that by relying on visualization you will turn into a rigid robot that is strictly and mindlessly programmed to follow one course of action. On the contrary, by using visualization you can actually become more adaptable and flexible in altering your workouts as needed. By tuning in more to your body, you can become more in touch with the signals your muscles are continually sending you. With this information, you can then create a mental program to meet what your body needs and can take.

All of the steps for using any form of mental imagery are the same. Since I have been referring to mental rehearsal so much, let's use it.

1. *Start from a base of relaxation.* Employ your own personal style to relax the mind and body. This process will put you in the studio where you can create your mental movies.
2. *Create the scene you wish to rehearse.* Use all of your senses in creating a very detailed picture of the event you wish to rehearse. See the weights, feel the coldness of the iron, hear the clanging of the plates, smell the sweet sweat of exertion, and even taste your hunger for growth! This may seem silly or irrational, but employing all of your mental senses activates

many sections of the brain so you can tell your body what you specifically want to do.

3. *Next, be in that scene you created.* Really feel yourself functioning in your visualization. You are no longer a passive observer, director, or producer of your mental movie, but you are now the actor or actress as well.

4. *Play out the sequence of events of your mental rehearsal.* Be very specific in experiencing every detail of your desired action. Feel the control and strength as you slowly lower the weights. Feel your muscles contracting, straining, but powerfully responding to the challenge. As you reach, say, the eighth rep, feel a pump or burn starting. Feel the confidence to push yourself through the last two reps with good form. After the set, feel your muscles aching wonderfully and be proud of your efforts.

   It is important to play out your scenario in great detail, focusing both on the process (good form for each rep) as well as the end result (a pump or a feeling of satisfaction). Always end the visualization on a really positive note. Your mental rehearsals are not a time to hold back. Be super positive! If you have problems focusing both on the process and the outcome at the same time, I have found it beneficial then to just tune in to the positive outcome.

5. *Repeat and refine your mental rehearsals as needed.* Just as exercising your muscles makes them more powerful, so does practicing your mental rehearsals make them more effective. Feel free to modify and refine your rehearsals so that they stay relevant to what you need to do. Become so familiar with your mental rehearsals that they almost become second nature to you.

By following this sequence you will soon find how easy and even fun mental rehearsal can be. And by regularly employing mental rehearsal in your workouts, you will also discover how strong and effective a mind-body link you can attain.

Years ago, when I first started researching all the applications of mental imagery in sports, I stressed how beneficial it could be for bodybuilders. At that time, many viewed visualization as a nice, but nonessential, luxury. Today, I propose that if you are not regularly employing various forms of mental imagery in each training session, you are falling behind your peers and, more importantly, behind your dreams.

Checklist

I realize I introduced a lot of technical information to you in this chapter. You may need to reread it a couple times to really understand and appreciate the power of this material. It will be well worth your time if you do so. Regularly utilizing the mind's eye is one of the most simple and effective things you can do to get more out of your training, but you have to understand the basic principles behind mental imagery.

In order to give yourself a better idea of what you understand and what you need to review, circle your response to each of the following questions. In the parentheses after each question is the page number where this topic was discussed.

- Seventy-one percent of all new information we receive comes through our sense of touch. We need to touch something so it will become real to us.
  yes   no   (83)
- Using the mind's eye is a foreign process that has little application outside the gym.
  yes   no   (83–84)
- I have no control when I use disassociative imagery. Some deeper mental function causes me to space out.
  yes   no   (86)
- Associative imagery is also known as mental anesthesia.
  yes   no   (85)
- One factor that seems to separate elite athletes of all kinds from good ones is that elite athletes regularly disassociate from themselves and the event.
  yes   no   (87)
- The best research support for using mental rehearsal is that the higher lobes of the brain cannot differentiate between something that is being very vividly visualized versus something that is actually occurring.
  yes   no   (88)
- The three specific components of mental rehearsal are called mental preplay, mental replay, and mental postplay.
  yes   no   (90)
- Mental rehearsal can effectively be used only before or after a workout.
  yes   no   (90–92)

- When creating my mental scene, I need to remain objective.
  yes   no   (93)
- Once you have created a visualization, you must always apply it precisely as it has been programmed so you will achieve the specific results.
  yes   no   (93)

If you answered "yes" to any of the above questions, then go back to that page in the chapter where it was discussed. Understanding mental imagery is essential to applying it effectively.

As you experiment with applying the different forms of mental imagery, you will be pleasantly surprised at how easy and natural they are. After a while, you might even ask yourself how you ever progressed in your training without them. They are that important.

The main points I learned—or was reminded of—from this chapter were:

1. _____ .

2. _____ .

3. _____ .

4. _____ .

What is the one point I will apply or practice during the next forty-eight hours (list the days here: _____
_____)

during my workouts? _____

_____ .

May your mental rehearsals become the visual and kinesthetic previews to turn your dreams into reality!

7

Affirmations

W e talk to ourselves all the time. Although very few of us are aware of it, we are always conducting an inner conversation with ourselves about ourselves. This inner conversation is called *self-statements*.

In self-statements we tell ourselves about ourselves or about the situations we are in. These statements are active representations of our belief systems. Self-statements can take two forms: negative self-statements (called put-downs) or positive self-statements (called affirmations). Properly understood and applied, our positive self-statements can channel a great deal of intensity into our training. This chapter will explore how you can become more aware of your self-statements, control your put-downs, and use positive affirmations in your training.

The physiological and psychological sciences have recently confirmed that the body and the mind are designed to be positive. Especially with athletes, we respond most directly and quickly to positive stimuli and programming. Positive thoughts in the mind are understood and implemented very efficiently by the body.

However, the kinds of self-statements most of us use in our everyday lives are negative ones. Just listen to some of these: "There is no way in the world I can lift that weight"; "Just look at my pitiful pecs"; "This is too uncomfortable today . . . I think I'll quit early"; "You wimp"; "I am a pencilneck"; and "I'm giving up." Sound familiar?

The types and sheer numbers of put-downs most of us use are nothing short of remarkable. It seems that many of us go out of our way to put ourselves down. Where successful bodybuilders will search for deficiencies in their bodies to correct them, put-down bodybuilders will search for deficiencies to drag themselves down even further. These people will make excuses, blame others, or blame the equipment, but in the end, they will always put themselves down.

Our self-statements can release a lot of energy into our training, but we first must learn how to stop these put-downs and properly construct positive self-statements.

Types of Put-Downs

The types of put-downs we use can be quite varied in scope. Some of the major types of bodybuilding put-downs include: (a) excessive worrying about how you are going to do (for example, "I hope I don't make a fool out of myself in front of everybody at the gym today"); (b) worrying about possible negative consequences ("When I am unable to lift this weight, everyone will laugh at me"); (c) being oversensitized to bodily reactions ("I'm so self-conscious that I am feeling nauseous"); (d) being very susceptible to distractions ("That idiot banging the weights around is preventing me from having a good workout"); (e) wondering and worrying how others are doing ("Gee, Charlie looks twice as big as me"); and (f) reflections of overall self-image ("I'm just a pitiful wimp").

Many of the put-downs we create are really quite devious in their subtlety. What we may initially be aware of as a passing thought, distraction, or idle comparison may really be a camouflage for a put-down. In any case, our put-downs serve only to sabotage our efforts and retard our progress.

The Power of Put-Downs

These put-downs have power over us because *we have been saying these things to ourselves in various ways for such a long time that we are no longer aware that we are telling ourselves these things anymore.* So in every similar situation we encounter, we automatically put ourselves down in the same old ways.

Here is an example. How many of you are not mechanically inclined? And how long have you been telling yourself that garbage? If you take the time to go back through your memory banks to find out the root cause of this "belief," it could be when you were eight years old and your dad laughed at you when you couldn't fix your bicycle, or when you were six and you were too weak to turn a bolt! You then concluded that you were not mechanically inclined and would never be so. Hence, the more you concluded that you were not mechanical, the more you generalized this belief into every mechanical situation you have since encountered. In essence, you learned how to give up.

What was really happening was that you started allowing fears of failure, risk, rejection, and embarrassment to dictate what you were to be. Ever since you concluded that you were not mechanically inclined, a little part of the left hemisphere of your brain has gone out to prove it. The subsequent failures merely strengthened the belief and paved the way for more put-downs. So, "See, I knew I couldn't do it," soon became your battle cry!

I   This was just one example of how we hold ourselves back by reinforcing our put-downs. If you take the time to search your beliefs for other such put-downs, you may be astounded at what you would find. You might come up with such put-downs as, "I am not coordinated," "I don't have the genetics for big deltoids," or "I am not intelligent enough to concentrate well." You may have been telling yourself these things for so long that you are barely aware that you are saying them anymore.

What Our Bodies Really Hear

Although we may believe our put-downs, our exaggerations, or our fears, our bodies are hearing quite a different thing. Our bodies are very trusting entities. They take things quite literally. Nowhere is the power of negative self-statements more profound than in how our put-downs are manifested in our bodies.

For example, I know many people, including bodybuilders, who say to themselves, "I feel like I'm carrying the world on my shoulders." These people also seem to have terrible postures and are susceptible to neck and upper-back problems. Is this a coincidence? Probably.

But maybe not.

I have worked with some bodybuilders who put themselves down by saying, "I don't have the backbone for tough workouts." These are also the people who seem to have more spinal problems or have underdeveloped lats. Coincidence? Probably.

But maybe not.

Over the last six years I have been working with female athletes and performing artists (including bodybuilders) who have an eating disorder called bulimarexia. This disorder occurs mostly in women and is characterized by binge eating, feeling really guilty about it, and then vomiting the food. Some women go through this cycle three, four, and even eight times a day. Every one of these women—and there have been sixty-six of them now—has said this about herself: "I just can't stomach that about me." And they don't. Coincidence? Probably.

But maybe not.

Here are some other daily examples of what we say to ourselves: "My boss is a pain in the neck" (or some other part of the anatomy!). "My heart just isn't in it today." "I was so mad I couldn't see straight." "I won't hear of it." "He gets under my skin." "I have no guts." Is it beyond coincidence when we get some kind of affliction that corresponds to our self-statements?

An increasing body of knowledge says that these statements and bodily reactions are beyond coincidence. As proof, ask yourself this: "How much of me has ever *heard* of me?" This is a tough question, so ponder it for a while.

My left index finger has never heard of a Kubistant. Neither has my right ankle. Nor have even my quads. There is only a little portion of my brain—about two cubic inches—that has ever "heard" of me.

So, when I am putting myself down, that little portion of my brain hears it as an analogy, an exaggeration, or a metaphor. *But the rest of me hears these statements as commands!* And the body, being the very trusting organism it is, seeks to put these commands into actuality!

The body takes things very literally. Like the fertile earth, the body *does not care* what you implant with your beliefs and self-statements. It will nurture and grow either weeds or wheat.

So, for better or for worse, for strength or for weakness, you really do become what you think about. That's why we have to be careful of what we implant with our self-statements. Our bodies deserve the best. This means that we have to make sure that our minds provide the best.

Transforming Put-Downs

You might be now saying to yourself, "All this is interesting, but what has this to do with bodybuilding?" Everything! Remember, our self-statements have a great influence in programming our bodies so we must make sure they are structured in productive and positive ways.

So how do you get rid of your put-downs? The goal is not to eliminate them. You are then only losing precious energy. Rather, the goal in handling put-downs is to transform and redirect the energy used for them into positive self-statements.

Bodybuilders must learn how to break down their negative self-statements and put them back together in more appropriate ways. Merely trying to think positively on top of a base of skepticism, fear, and put-downs does not work. You must actively transform your put-downs. Here's how:

1. Become aware of your specific put-downs. After all, you cannot change what you are unaware of. You might want to carry around a little notebook for a week and record all the put-downs you find yourself saying. Just objectively record them. Here is a hint: When you become aware of a put-down, avoid saying something like, "You're such a dummy for putting

yourself down like this.'' This comment only perpetuates the negative pattern! After a week or so of recording your put-downs, I think you will be surprised at how many you discover and how pervasive they are.

2. Construct phrases that actively challenge these put-downs. Remember, these negative self-statements are powerful when they are left unchecked. So, for example, the put-down, ''I'll never have big pecs,'' you might actively challenge by saying to yourself, ''Who says so? They are much bigger than they were last year.'' Or to the put-down, ''I always give up too soon,'' you may respond, ''Okay, the next time I am tempted to stop, I will pump out two more reps. I will endure.'' Or the put-down, ''Chris lifts much more than I,'' you might challenge by saying, ''Good for Chris! I will focus on what I can do.''

The more you actively call yourself on these put-downs, the more you will discover how really fragile and even absurd they are. Each time you become aware of a put-down, compliment yourself, stop whatever you are doing, and actively challenge the negative statement by replacing it with a more productive self-statement.

3. Once you have challenged these negative self-statements, you will then be in a position to reorient your thinking to focus on what you are and can do, instead of what you are not and cannot do. As you do, you will be more able to replace your negative self-statements with positive ones. At this point, you will be ready to construct affirmations.

Affirmations

Positive and productive self-statements are called affirmations. Affirmations are not wishes or hopes, nor are they boasts. Rather, they affirm or confirm those qualities and beliefs you already have. Affirmations open up and direct your energies so that you can focus your efforts. They are concrete reminders of those qualities, skills, attributes, and experiences that you already possess.

There are three general forms of affirmations: basic, bodybuilding-specific, and process. Each has its own special applications. Let's explore each in more detail.

Basic Affirmations

Basic affirmations are general, positive self-statements that can be used almost anytime. Here are some examples:

- "Everyday in every way I am better and better."
- "I am the captain of my ship; I am the master of my fate."
- "I like myself."
- "I trust my abilities."
- "I am relaxed."
- "I am enjoying what I am doing."
- "Sure I can."
- "I am on my side."
- "I can do anything I choose to do."

Fill in other basic affirmations that apply to you:

- _____
- _____
- _____
- _____

Basic affirmations are used to keep us relaxed, centered, and in touch with our positive and productive energies. It is best to use basic affirmations when you are relaxing or whenever any fears or doubts creep into your mind.

Bodybuilding-Specific Affirmations

These affirmations are used to remind and reinforce our specific bodybuilding skills and attributes. Here are some examples:

- "I am a serious bodybuilder."
- "I am a dedicated and determined bodybuilder."
- "I am a courageous bodybuilder."
- "I am a creative bodybuilder."
- "I am a persistent bodybuilder."
- "I am an intense bodybuilder."
- "I am an intelligent bodybuilder."
- "I am a bodybuilder."

Fill in other bodybuilding affirmations that apply to you:

- "I am a _____ bodybuilder."
- "I am a _____ bodybuilder."
- "I am a _____ bodybuilder."
- "I am a _____ bodybuilder."

It is best to use these bodybuilding-specific affirmations immediately before a workout, when you need to summon up more intensity, and immediately after a workout, to enhance the good feelings and sense of accomplishment.

Process Affirmations

Process affirmations consist of one or two words you can say to yourself in the midst of a workout. They are used to quiet and focus the mind as well as draw upon additional energies. Here are some examples:

- "Yes."
- "Through it."
- "Smooth."
- "Now."
- "Concentrate."
- "Easy."
- "Slow."
- "Strong."
- "Grow."
- "Focus."

- "Form."
- "Blow it out."
- "Explode."
- "Fire."
- "Bust it."
- "Attack."

- "Pump."
- "Good."
- "Go."
- "C'mon."
- "Do it."
- "Great."

Fill in other process affirmations that apply to you:

- _____
- _____

- _____
- _____

You can use these process affirmations both in your planning and in your mental rehearsing before a workout as well as during the workout. It has been my experience that softer-sounding process affirmations such as "yes" and "form" work better prior to training or early in the set. The more forceful-sounding process affirmations such as "blast it" and "explode" work better later in the set or workout when you really need to push.

Like the various forms of visualization, use all of these forms of affirmations at different times during the workout. Continually use, refine, and change your affirmations so that they always remain positive and appropriate to what you are planning and doing.

Positive affirmations are a great way to exude your positiveness and remind yourself of your good qualities. They make you better able to release and channel your energies into consistent and intense training sessions.

The System of Affirmations

Affirmations really do work. Learn to employ your own basic, bodybuilding-specific, and process affirmations regularly before and during your workouts. It is not hard to do. You are always making self-statements anyway, so why not make them positive? Saying affirmations can actually become a catalyst in focusing your mind on your training.

It is essential to construct your affirmations properly so that your mind and body will be able to understand them easily. Poorly constructed affirmations lose much of their punch and may even be an opening for negative put-downs to rush in. Here are the guidelines for constructing powerful affirmations:

1. *Make sure you have redirected your negative put-downs.* Remember, trying to place affirmations on top of a base of put-downs does not work. Continually monitor yourself so that as you discover new put-downs, you can immediately challenge and redirect them.

2. As with visualization, *achieve a relaxed state of mind.* Relaxation is home base. Being relaxed will open up the mental pathways to those attributes you wish to affirm.

3. *Construct your affirmations in a totally positive way* without qualifications or exceptions. Say, "I am a conscientious body-builder," instead of, "On every third Thursday when the gym isn't crowded and my biorhythms are on good days, sometimes I am not too bad of a bodybuilder, sort of!" Now, what kind of positive reinforcer is this latter example? Be directly positive. Period.

   Be especially careful to phrase your affirmations without using negative words. It is a little-known psychological and physiological fact that *the basal parts of the brain and the central nervous system cannot hear negative words.* So, if I say to myself, "I do not have small delts," "I am not reluctant to do that exercise," or "I will not give up today," what my brain and central nervous system are really hearing is, "I do have small delts," "I am   reluctant to do that exercise," and "I will   give up today!" Construct your affirmations not in terms of what you do not want to do (I know, I know, I used negatives there!), but rather in terms of the positive and productive things you want to do.

4. As much as possible, *construct your affirmations in the present tense*. We do not have control over the past or the future. The only time period we can control is right here and now. Phrasing affirmations too much into the future turns them into wishing, hoping, and dreaming. So instead of saying, "I will win my state contest next July," say, "I trust myself that I am doing everything I can to be my best next July." Or instead of saying, "I will definitely bench-press 315 lbs. today," say, "I am a strong bench-presser and will give it my very best shot." Remember, affirmations remind us of those positive qualities we already possess. In order to become the best in the future, you have to maximize those qualities now.

5. Finally, *continually repeat your affirmations and really believe them*. Our affirmations become stronger the more we use them. Feel free to modify existing affirmations or create new ones as necessary. Repeat, rely, and even revel in being positive!

Affirming and visualizing go hand in hand. Once you fully understand each approach, you can easily integrate them. So, for example, when you are visualizing the positive effects of an upcoming set of squats, you can also use the specific affirmation of, "I am a determined bodybuilder," or the process affirmation of, "Blast it," to strengthen the impact of the image.

Expand your bodybuilding affirmations into the rest of your life. Your bodybuilding affirmations will be weak if you continue to put yourself down in the other areas of your life. The more you affirm yourself, the more you will sincerely believe in yourself. And then, watch out! You will release the energy of your own "Incredible Hulk!"

Use the following checklist to assess your understanding of self-statements. Put a check by those points you understand and put a star by those points you need to review and apply more.

_____ • I am aware of my put-downs both in my bodybuilding as well as in the rest of my life.

_____ • My body literally hears and seeks to bring into reality what I say to myself about myself.

_____ • The goal is not to eliminate my put-downs, but to redirect the energy to transform them into positive self-statements.

_____ • Affirmations are not wishing, hoping, or boasting.

Affirmations simply, yet powerfully, remind me of and reinforce those qualities and experiences I already possess.

_____ • I understand the individual uses and applications of basic, specific, and process affirmations.

_____ • I understand that the way I construct my affirmations is as important as the affirmations themselves.

The main points I learned—or was reminded of—from this chapter were:

1. _____ .

2. _____ .

3. _____ .

4. _____ .

What is the one point I will apply or practice during the next forty-eight hours (list the days here: _____

_____)

during my workouts? _____

_____ .

I can do anything I choose to do!

8

Workout Issues

*N*o matter how well you prepare for a workout there will always be a multiplicity of variables during the actual training which you will have to address and respond to. Crowded gyms, your position in your training cycle, changing priorities, lapses in concentration, distractions, and recuperation time are just some of the factors to which you must constantly attend in order to consistently maximize your training sessions.

Bodybuilders who make the most steady gains are the ones who are able to combine solid planning with the necessary adjustments in their workouts. They have a picture of their goals and how they want to accomplish them, but they realize that they must remain flexible to keep their efforts appropriate to what their bodies need at the moment. This is what I call the "tight-loose property" of bodybuilding. Their goals are tight in providing specific plans, but they are also loose in providing adaptable approaches to keep the training effective.

This chapter will explore the psychological components of the major workout variables. As each bodybuilder is different, so is each workout. Continually remind yourself of the important issues in your training. By doing so, you will be better able to keep your workouts relevant and your progress consistent.

The Wisdom of the Body

It is almost a cliché, but the best bodybuilders really do listen to their bodies. Before, during, and after workouts they listen for messages from their bodies that provide them with information they can use in future planning. Our bodies possess a great deal of wisdom, and by listening to the feedback our bodies constantly send us, we can keep our workouts appropriate to what our bodies need and can handle. In this way, we can maximize each training session while minimizing the possibilities of overtraining or injury.

It is important to continually scan your body searching for sources of feedback. With this information you can then structure and modify your training accordingly. Evaluating previous sessions and planning for the next go hand in hand. You are wasting your time if you listen to your body and do nothing with this information. Listen and plan accordingly.

I have found it important to tune into not only the muscles you are working, but also the complementary muscle groups (such as triceps when you are working your biceps or hamstrings when you are working your quadriceps) so you can gain complete information. Really listen to your body. It has a lot to say!

Stretching

An excellent time to begin listening to your body is during your stretching before the workout. Stretching not only loosens up

muscles and surrounding tendons and ligaments, it also gives you indications of how well you have recuperated and how far you can push particular muscles during the upcoming workout.

Now, it is my guess that only about 20 percent of you do any regular stretching before a workout. You, no doubt, have many imaginative reasons for not stretching such as, "I only have enough time for the workout," "I'll take the first couple of sets easy instead of stretching," "I look foolish when I'm stretching," "I'll stretch twice as much tomorrow," and my personal favorite, "I stretch when I yawn!" And then we wonder why we get injured early in a set, or why our bodies never really feel in a workout.

You must convince yourself that stretching, like relaxing, is not a waste of time, but an investment in your time. Stretching is a wonderful way not only to warm up your muscles, but to warm up your mind as well. Stretching is an effective method to ease yourself into a workout so that you can really control each rep.

There is a neat sensing device in each major muscle group's connecting tendons that is called the Golgi Tendon Organ (GTO). It is an inhibitory device that protects muscles from becoming over-extended and injured. The GTO is activated when it stretches too far during overcontraction of the muscles. Once activated, the GTO partially or completely shuts down that muscle and sends signals to the brain to activate other—often complementary—muscle groups to compensate. If you continue trying to exercise the muscle after the GTO has been activated, the muscle is rarely fully stimulated. In addition, you run the risk of getting injured since other unrelated muscle groups have become involved.

Easy warm-ups and stretching before a workout have been shown to retard the GTO so the muscle can be more fully and safely stimulated. Stretching prepares the body to safely extend itself. Seen in this way, stretching plays an integral part in maximizing muscle stimulation.

Stretching is also beneficial in preparing the mind. During my stretching I can do many related things at the same time. I relax, rehearse my plan and sequence of exercises, mentally preplay how I want particular muscles to feel, and begin to focus my concentration just on me. So, by the time I start my first set, my mind and body are already in high gear and prepared for the rigors of the workout.

It has recently been shown that the best sequence in which to stretch is first to warm up by a little easy running, hopping, or walking. This gently warms up the muscles and slightly elevates the heart rate, so that when you begin the actual stretching, you can more effectively stretch the muscles and the connecting tendons and ligaments.

The best way to stretch is to let the position and gravity do the stretching for you. Do not force or bounce.This is not stretching. Effective stretching is static. Hold that position for twenty to thirty seconds until you almost hear the muscles ease off and say "ahhhh." Then you can slowly come out of that position.

Just as in the sequence of exercising muscles, I have found it effective to stretch my larger muscle groups first and my smaller muscle groups last. So I initially stretch my back and chest, lower back and abs, legs, and finally my shoulders and arms. I pay particular attention to fully warming up and stretching my lower back, shoulders, and neck because they take a lot of indirect pressure when I am exercising other muscle groups.

An increasing number of bodybuilders also stretch after a workout. Instead of rushing to the showers or for some liquid refreshment, these bodybuilders do some easy stretching. Remember, stretching is most effective when the muscles are warm, and they are definitely warm right after a workout. Stretching at this time promotes quicker recuperation of your muscles. Also, just as stretching before eases the mind and body into a workout, stretching after eases the mind and body out of the workout. Stretching after a workout provides you with a nice transition time so that you can assess and appreciate what you have accomplished during that training session. Some bodybuilders I know say that regular stretching following a workout is a key to putting in consistent training. You may want to experiment with this approach.

Of all of the workout issues, regular stretching is the one that will facilitate more dramatic progress. Stretching is the essence of listening to your body.

On Not Counting Reps

One of the effective adjustments I have made in the way I currently approach my training is that I no longer count reps during a set. I found that by not counting reps I can better monitor how I am stimulating the muscles being worked and make quicker and more appropriate adjustments. Beyond that, by not counting reps I can better feel myself in my muscles.

When I was counting reps, I would too often focus on the number I was on or worry about reaching my predetermined goal rather than listen to the muscles being worked. This was a no-win situation for me because if I didn't reach that number, I would feel bad. Conversely, quite often when I did reach that number, I would also feel bad because deep down inside me I knew I really could have done a couple more reps. In either case, I felt that I was not getting the most out of a set.

Now, I really tune into the muscles being worked. I focus on the deep stimulation of the inner fibers of the muscle. I find that as I do, I can also better monitor my form. When I sense that I am losing my form, I do only one or two more reps. In this way I can attain a good stimulation of the muscles without risking injury or bringing in unrelated muscle groups to help out. When I push myself so far that unrelated muscle groups have to help, I am not really exercising the muscle I intended. Not counting reps keeps me focused on the specific muscles I want to work.

The body can really go much further than the mind believes. By not counting reps, you have the opportunity to maximize each set fully and safely.

Variety in Training

Just as in the rest of life, variety is the spice of bodybuilding. Sometimes our training routines become so routine that they turn into ruts. And soon these ruts turn into crevasses. We become chronically stiff and sore. We also become mentally stale and dull. During these times, energy and drive seem to be at a premium and our motivations to go to the gym mysteriously erode.

Continually varying our workouts keeps us both physically and mentally fresh. By employing variations of the split system (that is, working some muscle groups one day and other muscle groups the next), we can effectively work different muscle groups every day. Albert Beckles has said that he has never done the same workout twice. Every workout is a new and unique experience. He is always looking for new ways to vary his training depending on what his body needs at that particular time.

You see, part of the wisdom of the body is that it quickly learns how to adapt to the specific stress put on it (that is, lifting a weight in a particular way). This adaptation process is what causes muscle to grow in strength and size. However, if you keep doing the same routine and sequences, lifting the same weights, and even exercising at the same angles, your body will soon know what to expect. When it knows what to expect, it no longer is forced to adapt as much, so progress is slowed.

By continually altering your workouts, your body is forced to keep guessing and adapting. It then never knows what to expect. When your body is always guessing and adapting, it stays fresh.

The same thing can be applied to your mind. When you continually have to plan and modify new workouts and variations of exercises, your mind stays active and involved. You create new and unfamiliar challenges for yourself so that you are always striving toward something. When you are in this frame of mind, you stay eager and motivated.

Varying your workouts means that you are continually changing all aspects of them. Change the sequence of the exercises, the number of sets, the weights used, and even the positions and angle of each rep. Also essential in varying your workouts is incorporating such advanced training approaches as pyramiding, supersetting, stripping, pre-exhausting, and forced reps. All of these variations keep your muscles constantly adapting.

For example, one day I might use this routine to work my biceps: pyramid barbell curl—five sets, alternating dumbbell curl—four sets (with some forced reps the last two sets), and stripped concentration curls for three sets of three strips. Two days later when I work my biceps again, the routine may be like this: superset easy bar curls with straight barbell curls—four sets, pyramid easy bar preacher curls—five sets, and seated incline dumbbell curls—three sets.

Varying every workout also has to be viewed in terms of your position in your training cycle. Every training session should be specifically planned and executed in relation to your training cycle. It would be foolish to lift some really heavy weights when your training cycle directs you to be doing some cutting and shaping exercises. If you refer to your training log and keep in mind the big picture, each workout will then be a piece of the puzzle that will eventually create a whole picture.

I do not want to give the impression that by varying workouts bodybuilders should capriciously work out in some kind of random manner. Varying your training is a planned program to achieve steady gains as well as to remain fresh and motivated. These variations are really based on consistency. High levels of dedication, commitment, and persistence provide the consistency from which effective altering of workouts can occur. It may seem strange that consistency and variety go hand in hand, but they are complementary partners in promoting balanced muscle growth.

If you really look at it, every rep is a new and creative experience. The biomechanics and physiology of each rep are unique. Extending this notion to our overall workouts, we can see that by adding variety to every training session we can continually keep our muscles fresh and responsive. When this occurs we achieve significant growth. So season your workouts with the fragrant spice of variety!

Form

Almost all training books and magazine articles stress the absolute necessity of maintaining strict form during exercises. Proper form is the only way to ensure that you are isolating the muscles being worked. If the poundages you are lifting are at the expense of your form, you are really working against yourself. A childish ego has no place in progressive bodybuilding. Maintaining good form, especially during the last three reps of every set, is absolutely essential in achieving the kind of deep-muscle stimulation you desire.

It is important to realize that every repetition is a *biphasic* (two-phased) process. Neglecting either one of these phases will minimize your results. The phase most of us emphasize is the *concentric* phase, where we contract the muscle through lifting, pushing, or pulling. However, the phase where most of the muscle stimulation occurs is the *eccentric* phase, where we resist gravity as the weight returns to its starting position. I am continually amazed at how even some advanced bodybuilders ignore the eccentric phase and let the weight literally come crashing down. Asserting control in your training means emphasizing the eccentric phase of each rep.

Slow and controlled resistance as the weight comes down is what really stimulates the inner fibers of a muscle. I recommend taking twice as long to resist the weight coming down as it took you to push it up. For example, if it took you two seconds to bench-press the bar up, it should then take you a full four seconds to resist it coming down. This can be sheer agony, but it works wonders. Swaying, bouncing, dropping, swinging, and any other form of momentum are the enemies of control. Slow concentrated form is what stimulates real muscle growth.

Remember, you are in control of each and every repetition. You actively have to assert control. Follow your breathing for a couple of seconds, mentally preplay your next set, tune into the specific muscles, and do it. Concentrate on every rep.

Many bodybuilders have adopted the "three-fifths" philosophy of lifting a weight. This approach has been best promoted by Larry Scott, the first Mr. Olympia. Larry recommends that you should pump the weight only through the middle three-fifths of the muscles' range of motion. In the first fifth, where the muscle is extended, the tendons are really being worked. And the last fifth, where the muscle is fully contracted, has very little deep muscle stimulation. The middle three-fifths stimulate the muscle in its optimum range of motion. This zone keeps continuous tension on the muscle and produces a more intense burn. Just as every rep is a biphasic process, so can every workout be viewed as a biphasic process as well. The actual training session breaks down the muscles, but the real growth occurs during the rest phase after the workout, when the muscles are healing themselves. Through this healing they adapt by becoming more resistant to future stresses put on them. This is called strength.

Proper form in bodybuilding also implies giving individual muscle groups a chance to recuperate. Good bodybuilders will never work the same muscle groups two days in a row. They will work different muscle groups so that the original muscles will have the opportunity to fully recuperate. This is why it is so important to plan your workouts a week or two in advance.

Bodybuilding means body building, not body tearing down. Control your plans, your form, and even your ego so you will always give your muscles the chance to grow. If you do they will reward you with strength and size.

You are an artist, and the bars, weights, and machines are your tools. As an artist controls his brushes, hammers, and chisels, so must you control yourself so you can create the kind of body that is good enough to be framed.

Prioritizing Workouts

I hate pull-ups. And that's why I love them! I have learned to re-orient my thinking so that I really look forward to working my weak body parts and doing my weak exercises to the point where I can't wait to get to them!

Now, this approach is exactly the opposite of what most bodybuilders do. These people frequently put off their weak exercises and body parts in favor of working their favorite exercises and body parts. These types of people are called "tank top bodybuilders." Typically, these people's fronts and arms look great so they look especially terrific in a tank top. But on closer inspection, it becomes obvious that their backs, legs, and overall proportion are seriously lacking. These people have yet to learn the importance of prioritizing their workouts.

One obvious commonality I see among successful bodybuilders is that they really look forward to exercising their lagging muscles. Where the rest of us are more likely to put off or even cancel the weak exercises, good bodybuilders hit their weak parts early in the training session when they are more physically fresh and mentally eager. They know that if they can conquer that weak part, the rest of the workout will be a piece of cake.

Two or three hours is a long time to be in a gym. Mindful bodybuilders realize this is a test of their concentration, planning, and prioritizing. Not only do they work their weaker body parts first, but they also conserve some of their energy so that they can have the same—or even greater—intensity during the last set as they did on the first. Jerry Kramer, the famous guard for Lombardi's Green Bay Packers, said, "Fatigue makes cowards of us all." Mindful bodybuilders know this only too well. It is for this reason that they pace themselves so they can finish the workout on an up-note instead of barely surviving or, worse, having to cut short a training session. Sure, these people could show off early in a workout, but the only thing this does is waste precious mental and physical energy. Their pacing of their workouts shows that they are in control of themselves and are thus able to put in consistent quality sets.

Progressive bodybuilders not only have pride in their strong body parts, they also have pride in bringing weak parts up to par. Prioritizing workouts is often the difference between intense, purposeful training and mindlessly going through the motions.

Training Partners

One workout issue that needs some attention is the use and role of training partners. Using training partners is an efficient way to train. While one works, the other rests, spots, and inspires. Good regular training partners share the intensity, motivate each other, and push each other to new levels of development.

I would like to make the distinction between a spotter and a training partner. Spotters are people who merely protect you from injury. True training partners not only share your motives and drives, but also share your specific plans and goals. Training partners can combine their energies so that the whole achieved is really greater than the sum of the individual contributions.

It is nice to have training partners, but you have to understand how they are best utilized. Too many bodybuilders become dependent on one training partner, so if he or she doesn't show up for one workout, the person cuts short the session or aimlessly pumps away. Other people mistakenly believe that they must become carbon copies of their training partners, always lifting the same weights. For all these people, using training partners eventually becomes a liability rather than an asset.

Here are some ways to use training partners positively:

1. Have two or three regular training partners. This way you won't become overly dependent on one individual.
2. Plan a workout beforehand with your training partner. Map out the session so both of you know what to do next. In this way you both can effectively maximize your time.
3. Discuss with your training partner how you prefer to be inspired during a workout. Some people like to be yelled at, others like to be calmly encouraged, while still others like to quietly focus in on themselves.
4. Genuinely compliment, support, and reinforce your training partner throughout the workout. Make the sessions fun, challenging, and intense. By putting energy into your partner, you will find you have more energy for your own training.
5. If your partner doesn't show up, use that time creatively. Work on lagging body parts, experiment with different machines and exercises, or simply do what you had planned. These are good times to remind yourself that you need to rely on yourself. You may even want to work out regularly a couple of times a week on your own.

Properly used, training partners can be a tremendous boost in your progress. The energy, support, and encouragement can be wonderful incentives. However, remember to keep the use of a training partner in perspective. Your partner cannot pump the weight for you or make your muscles grow. Only you can do that.

Mental Lapses

There are two basic forms of mental lapses that occur to us during workouts. By better understanding them we can learn to minimize them or correct them more quickly.

Distractions

The potential distractions in a crowded gym abound. Becoming immune to them is a real test of your concentration. However, no matter how intense our concentration is there will be times when we do become distracted. Learning how to handle this is essential in putting in quality workouts.

The central key in handling distractions can be best summarized by the following question: "What are you at the gym to do . . . become distracted or train?" It is imperative that you focus not on what you don't want to do (that is, the distraction), but on what you want to do (that is, the next set). Always keep in mind why you are there.

We all occasionally become distracted during a workout. A sudden crash of the weights or someone asking you a question is inevitable. The important thing is to get back on track as quickly as possible. Close your eyes, take a couple of deep breaths, relax, and return to the state of mind you were in before the distraction. Realize that some people may need to grunt, breathe loudly, or play music. You do not have control of them, but you do have control of what you do with those distractions. Choose to focus in on what you need to do next.

By better handling distractions and staying focused on your training, you will eventually develop the kind of concentration that will make you almost immune to distractions. You will then be in your own little world. This is the essence of concentration.

Mental Sticking Points

There is an interesting psychological phenomenon that most bodybuilders experience about midway through a workout. I call it a "mental sticking point." This term is derived from the weight lifting concept, where about halfway through a lift—especially when the muscles are fatigued—the weight "sticks." If this point can be passed, the lift can be completed. There also seems to be a point in our workouts where we mentally stick. During this time our concentration fades, we start taking longer and longer rests between sets, we begin to daydream, our energy mysteriously ebbs, and our resolve to remain intense diminishes. As we encounter these mental sticking points, it is much easier to cut short the workout than to continue.

Mental sticking points most frequently occur somewhere between 52 and 65 percent of the way into a workout. This zone is beyond the halfway point (the psychological "point of no return"), but not yet to the two-thirds to three-fourths point, where the end of the workout comes into view and we can gain added incentives to finish. If we can make it through this zone, we then can put in some quality sets.

How do you overcome these mental sticking points? First, recognize that they might occur. They have their greatest effects when they creep up on the unsuspecting. Second, keep your workouts fresh and ever-changing. Mental sticking points thrive on familiar routines. Third, when you sense a mental sticking point coming on, use this as a reverse stimulus to really bear down and put in some intense sets. Realize that this is probably the worst point of the workout, and if you can bear down now, the rest of the training session will be easier and more satisfying.

Remember, you are the captain of your bodybuilding ship and you must always stay at the helm. You do not have control of the waters around you, but by staying on course you can become more immune to hitting the sandbars of distractions and mental sticking points. By focusing on what you need to do, you will arrive at the harbor of satisfying workouts.

Becoming Comfortable With Discomfort

A subtle factor that needs to be mastered in order to make consistent gains is learning how to become comfortable with discomfort. The body can frequently take much more than the mind believes it can. It is the mind that often gives up and it is the mind that has to learn how to persist.

It must be emphasized that there is an important distinction between discomfort and pain. Pain is physical feedback that you are hurting yourself. That old saying "no pain, no gain" is garbage. People who believe this will soon find themselves sitting out training sessions with injuries. Pain is a message from your body that something is wrong. Pushing yourself while in physical pain is not the mark of courage or machismo. It is the mark of stupidity.

On the other hand, discomfort is an indication that you are extending yourself into uncharted regions of development. Discomfort has some physical components such as a burn or fatigue, but discomfort is mainly mental. As we extend ourselves during a set, we become anxious of the unknown. This combined with the feedback from our muscles often tempts us to quit. Oddly enough, these are precisely the times when we are achieving the best muscle stimulation.

Always be on the lookout for signs of pain, for they are sometimes hard to distinguish from discomfort. The more deeply you tune into yourself, the quicker and better you will be able to make this distinction. Once you discriminate that this is merely discomfort, commit yourself to push even further.

It may seem a little strange, or even masochistic, but learn to look forward to the discomfort. Remind yourself that this is when your inner muscle fibers are being best stimulated. Avoid the temptation of quitting a set in favor of doing an extra set later. Performing these last couple of reps will give you many more benefits than doing a whole extra set.

The first three-fourths of any set exercises the outer, more developed fibers of the muscle. It is only during the last couple of reps of the set, when these outer fibers become more fatigued, that the inner fibers begin to work. This is when the most complete muscle stimulation occurs that encourages subsequent growth.

Convince yourself that nothing worth achieving comes without a struggle. I am very wary of things I seem to achieve too easily. Our bodies like the status quo. Growth is uncomfortable and we have to push ourselves into these zones of discomfort. Then, and only then, are we maximizing our workouts.

Like mental sticking points, learn to use the signals of discomfort as reverse stimuli to bear down even further. Realize these are precisely the times when your previous work is beginning to pay off. Maintain strict form, slow the eccentric phase of each rep, and really tune your muscles.

The uncomfortable times can be seen as tests of the depths of your positive mental attitude. These are times when you need to be super positive and intense. Become even more eager and attack the last couple of reps!

Learn to become comfortable in this zone of discomfort. Genuinely look forward to it and make it a challenge. After all, you are training in order to grow, and growth is not easy. You must be able to push and endure with your mind before you can completely push and endure with your body.

Create the kind of "exquisite agony" that will make you proud!

The System of Mastering Workout Issues

This chapter has discussed some of the major workout issues that you need to be aware of and address. List here those issues you really need to work on:

1. _____
2. _____
3. _____
4. _____

What other workout issues did this chapter stimulate in your mind?

1. _____
2. _____
3. _____
4. _____

You may want to go back to the assessment in chapter 1 for ideas of other issues that might be retarding your training.

Check those items below that retard your workouts:

_____ • I do not stretch before a workout.
_____ • I do not stretch after a workout.
_____ • I tend to be too bound up in counting repetitions instead of tuning into the muscles being worked.
_____ • I do not vary my training enough.
_____ • I do not pay enough attention to my form.
_____ • I sacrifice quality for quantity.
_____ • I tend to bounce, swing, or drop the weights.
_____ • I rarely allow myself enough time to recuperate from a workout.
_____ • I do not work my weaker, less developed muscle groups early in the workout.
_____ • I rely too much on a training partner.
_____ • I am very susceptible to distractions in the gym.
_____ • I do not recover quickly from distractions.

_____   • I am susceptible to mental sticking points. They usually occur in my workouts during

_____

_____ .

_____   • I believe in "no pain, no gain."
_____   • I give up too soon when I experience discomfort.
_____   • Other: _____ .
_____   • Other: _____ .

You may also want to write down in your training log the issues, stumbling blocks, and lapses that are holding you back. After you do so, write down how you have tried to overcome them in the past. Finally, write down the plan you will use the next time you encounter one of these blocks.

Just as our bodies and training continually change, so do the psychological issues in our workouts. Learn to become aware of them, actively address them, and nip them in the bud.

Handling the mental issues of your workouts is a challenge that requires continual attention. Use your experience, creativity, adaptability, and just plain common sense to stay on top of your training.

Your mind dictates just how far, and in which directions, your bodybuilding will go. Each time you address a workout issue successfully or overcome a mental stumbling block, you improve your mind. And each time you improve your mind, you allow your body to extend itself. This is the ever-spiraling process of mindful bodybuilding.

The main points I learned—or was reminded of—from this chapter were:

1. _____ .

2. _____ .

3. _____ .

4. _____ .

What is the one point I will apply or practice during the next forty-eight hours (list the days here: _____)

during my workouts? _____

_____ .

The mind is the key to growth. You have the key, so use it to unlock the doors of development!

9
Competing

*S*o you carved out a pretty good body and you have been thinking you just might enter a competition to see how you fare against other bodybuilders? After one has been training seriously for a while, it seems that the next logical step is to compete.

Bodybuilding is not only a complete fitness activity, it can also be a wonderful performance and competitive sport as well. Competition is a valuable proving ground where one can not only achieve tangible results but also obtain specific feedback and perspectives to use in future training.

So competition can serve many functions. But do you have to compete? No, not at all. There seems to be a tendency promoted by the popular bodybuilding magazines that competition should be a natural extension of training. This is not the case. It is my guess that only about one percent of all those who train with weights ever compete. In fact, I know many wonderful and accomplished bodybuilders who choose not to compete. It is not because of lack of goals or fear of failure. It is just because they choose to focus on their training, for this is where they find the greater value. These people are very satisfied, striving for the internal goals they have constructed. Competition simply does not fit into their goals. So you do not have to compete.

However, for those of you who choose to compete, this chapter will present the major components necessary to maximize your competitive experiences. Even if you have no desire ever to compete, you can adapt what is presented into other performance areas of your life, such as giving a business presentation, taking a test, or competing in other sports. Competing can be satisfying and even fun, but it can be much more so if you master these major components.

Before Your First Contest

Competition is much more than just strutting your stuff, collecting your trophy, and going home to bask in glory. There are a myriad of performance variables, factors, and psychological intangibles that you need to be aware of so you can achieve the most out of every competition.

If you have chosen to compete, congratulations. You have no doubt displayed the commitment and determination that has resulted in a body of which you are proud. Before you throw yourself into your first competitive journey, you may want to ask yourself this simple question, "Just why do I want to compete?" If you come up with such answers as, "because all my friends are," "because I should," "for glory and rewards," or "I don't know," you may want to delay your entry into the world of competition, for you will probably have a disappointing experience. You need to have more clear-cut goals that competing can fulfill. If your answers to the question were, "to excel in a new personal arena," "to compare and contrast myself with others," or "to set new standards for myself and experience new things," then you will be approaching competition with the proper frame of mind.

My first running road race was a marathon. I had been told that I should have many shorter races under my belt before attempting the rigors of a marathon. I figured running was running, and I would save myself for the marathon. Well, thankfully I survived, but I should have listened to the advice and gained a little experience prior to any major performance.

In the same way, many bodybuilders make the mistake of rushing into their first contest before they have any idea of what they are doing or what is necessary in order to perform well. The results are usually obvious mistakes, disappointment, and even embarrassment.

Before you enter your first contest, it is a good idea to observe a couple of contests. Get a feel for the atmosphere, the sequence of events, the pressures on the competitors and how they react to them, and the details that need to be mastered. Note the good as well as bad presentation points of the competitors.

It is also a good idea to jot down notes on what you observe. There are so many fine points and intangibles that the only way you will remember them is if you take notes. Some items you may want to record are: posing variations, stage presence (posing as well as waiting to pose), posing suit styles and colors, tanning, lighting, positioning (especially during the posedown), music selections, sequence of poses, hiding weak points, and relating to the audience.

By observing a couple of contests, you can acquire a good feel for how it will be when you compete. This prior exposure will be valuable in helping you be more relaxed. These observations really set the foundation for applying the success principle called "Other People's Experience." By using other people's experiences, you can accelerate your own learning curve and be better able to avoid basic mistakes as well as benefit from good examples.

A cornerstone of employing other people's experiences is realizing that there is an important distinction between adopting what you see versus adapting it. Adopting is trying to copy and replicate others' styles. This rarely works because you are trying to mold yourself to others' personal styles instead of modifying these styles to your own. This latter approach is called adapting. Adapt what you observe to create your own unique style. By developing your own style, by adapting bits and pieces of others' styles, you will create a performance image that is you.

Using all of the information you attained, start developing your own game plan for your first competition. Choose a local or state contest in which you want to compete. Make sure you take care of all the logistical considerations first, for failing to do this often causes a lot of stress and wastes precious energy as contest time approaches. Get your application in, learn the rules and regulations, confirm appearance times, make your travel and hotel reservations, and plot out your training time line.

Posing

It is one thing to have a great body. It is quite a different thing to present it effectively in a competitive situation. You can have the most massive and symmetrical body in the world, but if you cannot present it well, you will not achieve the kind of success you desire. Posing is a completely different and unique dimension of bodybuilding. In posing you have to put everything together and

present it in an effective package. Posing is very different from training and the dimension that is the most difficult to learn and refine.

Effective posing involves dynamically and fluidly presenting the
strong points of your body while covering up the weaker points.
To be successful at posing, you have to be genuinely proud of the
body you have created. Any fears, apprehensions, doubts, or insecurities will be reflected in your posing. Bodybuilders who are
unsure of themselves or their bodies will not present the kind of
posing line, image, and air of confidence that are necessary for a
successful performance. So the prerequisite to effective posing is
that you have to learn to believe in yourself, resolve insecurities,
be positive, and concentrate.

The Mandatory Poses

Learn the mandatory poses inside and out. Dissect each one of these
poses and learn the proper position of each muscle group involved.
More importantly, learn how each muscle group feels when
presented well in a particular pose. So, for example, in a side chest
pose, learn the arm and leg positions, but also learn how your pecs,
biceps, and even calf muscles should feel.

After you have become aware of the individual parts of each pose,
put them all together so you feel how to best present the whole

pose. Have pictures taken of you from all angles so you can see how to best present yourself. Become so used to each mandatory pose that when someone says "double biceps shot" you immediately properly pop into this pose.

Learn all the mandatory poses so completely that they become second nature to you. In a pressurized competitive situation there is a tendency for the mind to go blank. Having your mandatory poses so well ingrained in you will give you the reassurance that even if your mind does go blank, you will still automatically be able to hit effective mandatory poses.

Optional Poses

Your optional posing routine should present your best muscles and features as well as reflect a little of your personality. This sounds simple, but this is quite a tall order.

The first step in developing your routine is to observe the masters of posing. Watch seasoned competitors like Mohamad Makkay, Ed Corney, Carla Dunlap, Corrina Everson, and Albert Beckles. See how they present their best features while masking their weaker ones. Also observe how they flow from one pose to another, setting the mood or tone for the overall routine. Observe how they have choreographed precise movements to the music. Finally, see how they relate to the judges and audience and always finish with a bang.

Develop your unique style that represents who you are. Nothing is more personal than your body, so create the kinds of poses that reflect both your body and your personality.

Many novice competitors do not fully understand that each pose consists of three phases: the transition leading into the pose, the pose itself, and the movements leading out of the pose (which are also the transition into the next pose). Posing is a cyclical process that should flow easily together. It is these transitions that really give a good overall impression.

Save your best poses for the end of your routine. Realize that the last things you do are the first things the judges remember. An effective posing routine should not so much lead to one crescendo, but should include a series of crescendos. Give them a series—something to remember!

Be careful to choose music that fits your personality and the mood you wish to present. Feel free to splice together different segments. Just make sure the splicing job is good quality and the segments present a continuous effect. You may also want to bring at least two copies of your tape to the contest, for tape machines are notorious for eating them! Learn your music inside and out and then start fitting your poses to it.

Practice, practice, practice your posing. Perfect it to the point where you can do the whole routine automatically. Get as much feedback on your posing routine as you can. Enlist others' comments, have photos taken of you, and, if possible, videotape the whole routine. Perfect individual poses, but also emphasize the transition movements between each pose.

As your contest approaches, spend a greater proportion of your time on your posing. There really is not much more you can do to build up your muscles. Spend this time dieting and doing more aerobic exercises. Many novice competitors do not realize just how physically taxing posing is. Get to the point where you can hit poses for eight to ten minutes straight. You will be amazed at how slowly time goes by!

Many experienced competitors visualize themselves to be a certain kind of animal. They then become this animal during the posing routine. For example, many competitors visualize themselves as big cats, such as cheetahs or lions, that represent of the qualities of power and grace. Or some bodybuilders combine animals to better represent all of the qualities they wish to exude, such as a gorilla and a lion that symbolize mass with powerful proportion.

Whatever methods you use, learn your routine so well that you can actually free yourself up from the specifics to enjoy your posing. This is where your personality will come out. Then you will be ready to present yourself well.

As you learn to pose effectively, you will discover a special kind of pride in being able to pose well. Refined, stylish, and polished posing can overcome muscle deficiencies and imbalances. Good posing can be the difference between placing well and being an also-ran.

Nutrition and Dieting

Nowhere is the saying, "You are what you eat," more evident than in bodybuilding competition. The longer you have been bodybuilding, the more important the factor of nutrition becomes in developing and maintaining a proportioned body. At advanced

levels, nutrition may play an even bigger role than one's actual training approaches. Especially in competition, nutrition is *the* single greatest variable in determining whether or not a contestant will peak.

As a whole, bodybuilders are head and shoulders above their fellow athletes in the knowledge of nutrition. They have demystified much of the intricacies of nutrition and have been able to apply them to their daily lives. However, there still occasionally appears some kind of fad diet or supplement that takes bodybuilders off on counterproductive tangents. In order to really maximize your training and prepare yourself for competition, you must have a solid understanding of nutrition.

This section will present just a cursory overview of nutrition, especially as it relates to competition. There are many excellent sources that completely explore bodybuilding nutrition (see suggested readings). Learning about nutrition is an ongoing process so always be open to learning new dynamics.

Food As Fuel

We need to view what we eat as the fuel that runs not only our muscles, but the rest of our bodies and brains as well. We decide what quality of food we will ingest to fuel ourselves. We can choose a low-octane fuel found in most processed, fried, or fast foods and pay the physical and psychological prices for it. Or we can choose a high-octane fuel found in foods as close as possible to their natural states and benefit from it.

We have to continually be conscious of the foods we choose to eat. For every splurge or lapse, our bodies and our training will usually suffer for at least the next seventy-two hours. I am a vegetarian and on those rare occasions that I do eat meat—usually on pizza with friends—I pay the price for days afterwards. I not only have trouble digesting this food, but I also feel lethargic during my training. Even though I try to rationalize that this isn't "real" meat, my body knows better!

Our nutrition must always vary according to our training cycles. For example, in the summer when I run more than I weight train, my proportions of nutritional intake are as follows: 80 percent complex carbohydrates, 10 percent proteins, and 10 percent fats. My muscles need the fuel from the carbohydrates in order to endure the rigors of running, so I eat a lot of whole grains, vegetables, and fruits. During the winter when I am bodybuilding heavily, my proportions are as follows: 70 percent carbohydrates, 20 percent proteins, and 10 percent fats. My body needs a higher protein resource for muscle repair and growth, so I eat more eggs, nuts, and soups. Still, you can see that these proportions do not change much from one season to the next. Consistency of intake is the key. My body always knows what to expect in terms of fuel intake.

Getting a handle on your nutrition starts with, and continually depends on, your paying attention to it. We all have to create the right system of eating that is appropriate for our unique bodies. This means that what may be good for your training partner may not be good for you. Feel free to experiment, but always base your eating habits on what works for you.

Dieting

As you approach a contest, you would like to reduce your body's fat and water content as much as possible so your muscle definition can show through your skin. This is called *getting ripped*. Dieting is a physically and emotionally taxing process that must always be monitored in order to work.

Contestants need to diet, but not so much that they look like they have just been released from a concentration camp. Until recently, many bodybuilding contests—especially women's—have almost turned into a dieting rather than a muscle contest. This trend is gradually changing. Today, judges want to see clearly defined muscles, but they also want to see a healthy appearance.

Here are some guidelines to healthy and effective dieting:

- Many bodybuilders do not fully understand that losing body fat is a biphasic (two-phased) process. We must reduce the number of calories going in, but we also need to increase the number of calories being used. The best way to accomplish this is to increase the amount of aerobic exercise you do. Swimming, bicycling, or aerobicizing will burn up many calories without seriously affecting your muscle mass.

- It makes sense that the best way to diet is to always be in a position where you do not have to lose much weight. Maintain your training weight within 5 percent of your desired contest weight.

- The steady approach to dieting is best. Avoid anything, such as fasts in particular, that might shock the body. Slow, controlled, and sensible dieting is best in the long run.

- During your dieting remember that any food you ingest should be quality calories. I define quality calories as food that is close to its natural state and has minimum cooking preparation. Use the following rules of thumb in your nutritional intake. When you are in regular training, ingest 15 quality calories per pound of body weight each day. When you are dieting for a contest, ingest 10 calories per pound. So, for example, if you are a 100-pound female, you could ingest 1,500 calories during training and around 1,000 calories during contest dieting. If you are a 200-pound male, you could ingest a full 3,000 calories during training and around 2,000 calories during contest dieting. These contest dieting figures may appear high, but this is a safe and sane approach that has the best chance for success.

- Plan your dieting to take a full one to two weeks longer than you expect. Many novice bodybuilders usually hit their peaks three to seven days after the contest because their dieting did not really grab hold when they expected. I believe that it is better to reach your desired weight a couple of days early and then maintain it rather than reach it a couple of days too late.

- Judge your dieting not so much by how much you weigh, but how you look. Judges don't care about your weight. They want to see how well your muscles are defined.

- After the contest avoid binging. Just as you don't want to shock your body going into a diet, you don't want to shock your body coming out of it. Your recuperation will be greatly facilitated if you gradually regain your old eating habits and intake level.

- Finally, experience is a valuable guide. Learn from your mistakes as well as from your successes. Develop your own system of nutrition and dieting that has been proven to work for you.

Your body can be viewed as a dynamic laboratory. You must learn the proper ways to fuel your laboratory so it runs efficiently and effectively. Continually strive to learn about nutrition and implement these learnings so you will be able to show off a lean and ripped body.

Intangibles

A plethora of preparation intangibles must be addressed before the contest so you can perform well during the competition. Travel and hotel reservations, audiotaping, registration, posing suits, eating in a new city, tanning, and a number of other factors need to be attended to, so you can concentrate on your contest preparation and performance.

The best advice is to address all these factors as early as you can, so during the two weeks prior to a contest you can focus on your posing, dieting, and mental preparation. Attend to most of the factors yourself. I have found that letting a trusted friend or loved one take care of some of these factors tends to waste your energy because you spend extra time checking up on them or wondering when they are going to do the tasks. Handle these yourself and get back to your preparation.

If possible, well before the contest walk out on the stage on which you will be competing. Get a feel for the environment and especially for the lighting. Bright lights tend to bleach out the skin so make sure you achieve a good deep tan. You might also want to experiment with some artificial tanning techniques, but find out what combination of artificial and natural tanning works best for you. Do this experimenting two months or so before the contest. Trying to figure this out a week before the show will almost surely invite disaster.

Particularly in the gym before the competition, focus on conserving energy. Wear loose-fitting sweats to conceal yourself, avoid comparing yourself to other competitors, and go about doing the things you need to do. The combination of precontest tension and the stresses of dieting frequently make people do strange things. Plan and focus on you and the specific things you need to accomplish in order to be totally prepared for the contest.

The Actual Contest

The actual contest should be fun. View this as the frosting on your bodybuilding cake, the reward for all your sacrificing and preparing. This is the time for you to show the world what you have achieved!

Believe that you are there to give the best effort and present yourself in the best way possible. Recognize that you are not there to sabotage yourself, so trust that whatever you do is for the best. Genuinely believe in yourself and be on your side.

From the time you enter the auditorium for the prejudging, focus only on you. Don't make the mental error many novice competitors make of continually comparing, contrasting, and competing with others. This is a waste of precious energy and concentration. Be in your own little world.

Realize that some people may try to "psyche you out" by playing games, saying things to get a reaction, or trying any way to get under your skin. Understand that people who play such head games are trying to drag you down to their levels or are attempting to cover up their own inadequacies. Do not react to them. If you do, they have won. Concentrating on what you have to do will keep you immune from any such tactics. Be friendly, helpful, but always focus in on you.

An increasing number of contests span a couple of days so it is essential that you relax and conserve your energy. Recognize that a little tension is good. This is a sign that your body and mind are getting up for a significant effort. However, control your emotions as much as possible. Use your formal relaxation sequences, visualization, affirmations, and any little gimmicks you have to deflect the pressure. Use the pressure, don't let it use you.

After the contest, accumulate specific and honest feedback from a variety of sources. You may even want to contact some judges to receive their input and recommendations. Write down the things you need to emphasize or do differently next time. It has been my experience that the bodybuilders who improve upon their contest performances the most are the ones who have the honesty and courage to seek feedback. They view their efforts as learning experiences.

Most important of all, be proud of what you have done. You have pushed yourself into areas that few people ever do. Recognize that you are among an elite percentage of bodybuilders who have made the commitments and sacrifices and have taken the risks to compete. Pat yourself on your wide lats, take time to recuperate, and then start planning for the next contest!

Competing can be a marvelous way to add to your bodybuilding. It is both a personal proving ground and an objective performing arena that can enrich your entire life. If competing is not for you, fine. Continue doing the training you enjoy. But if competing is for you, give your best efforts, learn from your experiences, and apply them to becoming a better bodybuilder.

The System of Peaking

The concept of peaking always receives a lot of attention from competitive bodybuilders. However, they most often refer to it when they have missed their peaks. The quest for the peak has attained almost mystical proportions. For many competitors, hitting their peaks is like finding the Golden Fleece.

The vast majority of bodybuilders who miss their peaks have few clearly defined goals and no specific plans to achieve them. These people usually try to cram everything into the last month before a contest. The result is that they usually overtrain, look gaunt, and have polka dots from their tanning lotions!

There is nothing magical about peaking for a contest. Peaking is a planned and intelligent program that integrates the mind and body to produce a razor-sharp performance. Presenting the system of peaking is a good way to summarize this chapter on how to maximize the competitive experience.

1. It is essential that you choose a contest that is appropriate for you and your stage of development. Give yourself adequate time to train physically and prepare for it. Create a training cycle that culminates in the contest. Then plot out a time line that includes such factors as developing specific muscle groups, employing other exercises and activities, nutrition and dieting, posing, and mental preparation. Refer to chapter 3 to refresh yourself on time lines and training cycles.

    All of this planning will be useless until you commit yourself to the competition. You must give this contest a priority in your life. If you don't, you will be really working against yourself. Throw all of your bodybuilding eggs into one basket and give the entire process of peaking your best shot.

    A tunnel-visioned focus on your goals is essential. Keep in mind not only your plans, but your personal purpose in this quest as well. Making sacrifices goes hand in hand with any such commitment. Develop what Mike Mentzer calls a "controlled obsession" toward your training. This is a time that will test your concentration, endurance, and even patience. To sustain your intensity, keep in your mind's eye your vision of what you want to achieve.

As you proceed you might develop what Mentzer calls a "siege mentality" toward your whole life. You become so focused in on what you need to do that things irrelevant to that do not matter. Realize that this siege mentality is necessary for excellence, but it is temporary. After the contest you will have to compensate for those areas that were neglected. Remember, you have just one shot to peak, so give it your all.

2. The sequence of planning for a peak usually follows this general progression:

   - working on mass→working on symmetry and definition
   - quantity of weights lifted→quality of reps
   - emphasizing segments and individual body parts→emphasizing tie-ins and the whole body
   - longer rests between sets→shorter rests and more supersets
   - balanced nutrition→imbalanced nutrition for dieting
   - segmented posing→integrated posing including transitions
   - physical preparation→mental preparation

   Construct your time line in such a way that these different elements work together to achieve a unified result. This result is the peak.

3. It seems ludicrously obvious that once you have established your time line for your training you have to use it. But many bodybuilders establish time lines and then seem to disregard them! Slipping off onto counterproductive tangents is very easy, especially early in the training cycle. This lost time cannot be made up. Bodybuilders who use time lines have to understand the necessity of living with their priorities. Remember, planning means doing something with your plans.

   Using previous experiences in peaking, top bodybuilders have learned to pace themselves. In every aspect of their training they emphasize quality. Sure, they could show off during a training session, but this would only waste precious time and concentration. Mindful bodybuilders recognize that showing off now may prevent them from showing off well at the contest. They keep the big picture in mind and prioritize their efforts.

4. Feel free to adapt, alter, and modify your time lines so they remain appropriate. Refer to your time lines often and compare your planned progress with the actual progress. This will provide you with both the perspective and incentives to keep on going.

5. As you proceed into your training, increasingly apply your relaxing, visualizing, and affirming. These practices will not only be valuable in themselves, they will also help you maintain your composure and awareness so you will be better able to stay on course.

   Rely on these mental skills to channel any fears, doubts, and insecurities productively into your training. Remember, you have total control of who you will become and how you will present yourself. Relaxing, visualizing, and affirming should be like old reliable friends to you.

6. Most competitors believe that peaking should be a process of ever-increasing intensity culminating in one exploding crescendo. This process works for only a very few. For most of us, the best approach is to reach and refine our peaks through a process called *tapering*.

   Like an airplane landing, tapering uses all of the physical and mental preparation gained from the months of training to glide to the target. It is a time for easing off on some aspects of your training, but it is also a time for maintaining and even intensifying other aspects. For example, during the two weeks prior to a contest you should ease off on the heavy training, but increase the time and intensity of posing and mentally rehearsing the event.

   Just as in the early phases of your time lines, trust is a must during tapering. Recognize that at this point you cannot do much more to make significant improvement, but by trying harder because you mistrust yourself, you could seriously detract from your peak. Convince yourself that this planned course is your best shot to hit your peak.

7. Do everything well! Really emphasize all the positive aspects about you. Fear, anxiety, and stress can erode much of the physical training you have done. Focus on being genuinely positive in everything you do as you approach the contest date.

   Even though you still will have some faults and deficiencies, emphasize your strong points and what you do well. Your weaknesses will not improve at this point and there is nothing to be gained by reminding yourself of them. Rely on and be proud of your strong points.

The week before the contest, focus on relaxing and mentally rehearsing every little aspect of your performance. Actually become those qualities you wish to exude onstage. Be positive, eager, proud, strong, graceful, symmetrical, and a winner! Do not let doubts, fears, or other negative thoughts reside in your mind. Channel all your energies into being the best possible you.

From the time you enter the city or the auditorium, be a performer. Exude poise, confidence, control, and mastery at all times. It is illogical to expect that you will magically turn on poise and confidence onstage when you have been worried and negative offstage. Reinforce what you do well. Focus on who you are. And then go do it!

8. Finally, learn from your experience. Although every peak you achieve is unique, there are some necessary elements you need to produce your best efforts. Develop your own formula for peaking, so the next time you start the process it will seem like familiar territory. You will then be more efficient, for you will better know what to do.

Peaking is a wonderful process. It is a marvelous opportunity to combine all the physical, mental, nutritional, and performance parts of you into one unified whole. Not many people can commit themselves to planning a goal, much less carrying it through. Always be proud of what you accomplish.

May your bodybuilding peaks reward you with panoramic vistas and reveal new mountains to climb!

Competition Checklist

Check off below those points presented in this chapter that you understand and put a star by those points you need to work on.

_____ • I have committed myself to competing in a contest.
_____ • I have given myself the time to adequately prepare for the competition.
_____ • I have developed a detailed training cycle and time line to plot out my path.
_____ • I understand the basic format, sequence, and dynamics of competitions.

_____ • I understand what I have to do with my mandatory posing.

_____ • I understand what I have to do with my optional posing routine.

_____ • I have a good base for proper nutrition.

_____ • I have developed my own form of intelligent dieting.

_____ • I understand the competition intangibles that I have to attend to, such as audiotaping, entry applications, tanning, traveling, posing suit, and so on.

_____ • I have developed and rely on my own unique forms of relaxation, visualization, and affirmations.

_____ • I understand how to combine all of the variables needed to peak for the contest.

_____ • I believe in myself!

The main points I learned—or was reminded of—from this chapter were:

1. _____.

2. _____.

3. _____.

4. _____.

What is the one point I will apply or practice during the next forty-eight hours (list the days here: _____

_____)

during my workouts? _____

_____.

An intelligent, planned, and purposeful approach toward competing can make you a better bodybuilder as well as a more complete person.

10

The Modern Warriors

*F*rom ancient Japan to the frontiers of the Wild West existed a type of person who was renowned for his ferocity and skill in fighting. He was also feared and respected for his resourcefulness and ingenuity. He would frequently overcome great odds and accomplish the tasks of four men. He exhibited personal qualities that were envied by even his greatest adversaries. This person was the warrior.

The warrior was revered for his single-mindedness of purpose and his commitment to personal excellence. Mastery and dedication were his trademarks. He would endure great hardships to attain his goals and accomplish his mission. However, the warrior always put his achievements within a larger framework.

The warrior also exhibited a wholeness of living that, at first glance, seemed surprising from one so committed to duty and purpose. The warrior placed a great emphasis on advancing his culture, his family, his art, his spiritual pursuits, and his daily rituals. He aimed at achieving a state of completeness from which he could contribute to a greater whole.

The ancient warrior was purposeful, resourceful, and even noble. In many ways, he was an example of the highest levels of mastery and completeness that could be achieved by the human species. It could be said that the warrior was a phenomenon of his time and is an antiquated and even irrelevant concept in today's fast-paced, ever-changing, and specialized society.

I submit to you that the image of a warrior is appropriate and relevant in today's life. No, we don't have to carry swords or spears.

However, we can adapt some of the qualities exhibited by ancient warriors to broaden our modern-day lives. I have observed many warrior-like qualities in a variety of modern-day people, ranging from athletes, to performing artists, to business people, to working mothers. But perhaps nowhere do I see more qualities typified by the concept of the modern-day warrior than in the dedicated bodybuilder.

Many of today's conscientious bodybuilders live lives that would win approval from ancient warriors. Today's bodybuilders exhibit commitment, persistence, and a sense of purpose that is admirable. These people shatter the old stereotype of the musclehead by learning about and integrating into their training such diverse concepts as nutrition, kinesiology, and even psychology and creativity. These people also live lives that are characterized by balancing single-minded dedication with broader perspectives.

Now, not every bodybuilder is a warrior. Far from it. There are still a great number of the prototypical jocks and jockarinas who are ego-bound in having big chests and arms, or who are myopically immersed in how they will do in some kind of competition. These people are not warriors.

The bodybuilding warrior has progressed beyond these limited areas of weight training. He or she has expanded the roles and functions of training into a comprehensive and balanced lifestyle. These people use bodybuilding just as the ancient warriors used their rituals, tests, and training. For them, bodybuilding has become the symbolic glue that holds the rest of their life roles together. The dedication and commitment these people employ in their training can be applied to the rest of their lives in developing a bodybuilding lifestyle.

The Bodybuilding Lifestyle

Any experienced bodybuilder knows that the benefits of pumping iron extend into other areas of life. Confidence, poise, and pride are apparent in any bodybuilder you see on the street. It's clear that the same kinds of qualities you need to excel in bodybuilding can also be applied to excelling in the rest of your life. This expansion of the roles, uses, and benefits of pumping iron is the core of a bodybuilding lifestyle.

Now, a bodybuilding lifestyle is much more than going regularly to the gym four or even six days a week. A bodybuilding lifestyle implies that you are deeply committed to your training and have integrated it into your entire life. No, you don't have to live, eat, and breathe bodybuilding. On the contrary, you must develop the right perspective on bodybuilding so that your training fits into the larger picture of your life.

Those who have integrated the training into the rest of their lives are warriors. The modern-day bodybuilding warriors practice the same kind of discipline and control outside the gym as they do inside. It would be incongruous to be committed and persistent inside the gym while being sloppy, undisciplined, and excessive outside the gym. The incongruency would eventually adversely affect not only the training, but the overall quality of life as well.

Bodybuilding warriors understand that the only way to remain effective during their training is to have the rest of their lives consistent with their training lives. So they pay the same attention to details in their nutrition, careers or education, and relationships as they do in their training. Developing this sense of congruency and consistency provides the framework for effective workouts.

In their training, warriors continually vary their workouts and intensities, and they also vary how they use free weights, machines, and even the angles of individual repetitions. They participate in other sports and physical activities such as swimming, bicycling, and running. These other activities not only complement their body-building, they also facilitate a broader and more balanced perspective toward fitness and health.

Balancing and Juggling

Warriors balance their workout lives with the rest of their lives. Sure, their training is important and they give priority to it, but not to the exclusion of their other roles and responsibilities. They may temporarily neglect a portion of their lives—when they are peaking for a contest, for example—but constant neglect will eventually lead to a decline in their training effectiveness. Warriors understand that in order to give continued intensity and persistence to their workouts, they must have the rest of their lives in order.

True bodybuilding warriors integrate the training side of their lives with the personal, professional, emotional, and spiritual sides of their lives. They have found that as they attend to each of these areas, they actually have more energy and commitment for their training. Their bodies seem fresher and their minds more focused. Achieving an equilibrium, a balance in their lives, is essential for putting in consistently good workouts.

Bodybuilding warriors realize that they must continually find new ways to stay motivated and purposeful in all areas of their lives. If they neglect one aspect of their lives (for example, personal relationships) for long enough, eventually other areas of their lives will be affected, including their training. Warriors have been able to strike a balance between staying consistent in their daily duties and keeping an open mind to learning new things.

I've used the word *balancing* several times, but actually this term is becoming outdated. Balancing implies that a person has only two roles to keep in equilibrium. Today, our lives are much more complex than that. We must meet the needs and demands of numerous life roles. This is why I now prefer the term *juggling*.

If you juggle, or have ever really observed a juggler, you know that this is a fascinating activity. The juggler has to keep all the objects in a precise pattern while maintaining an overall rhythm among them. Once the rhythm is achieved, the juggling becomes almost automatic.

We can use juggling as a metaphor for effectively attending to our life roles. Say, for example, you have four balls in your hands. Each ball represents a major life role—your training, career or education, relationships, and spiritual roles, for example. As you juggle these balls, you will notice that at any one time there is only one ball in your hands. This is the only ball you can control. If, however, you keep a ball in your hand for too long (giving too much attention to your training side, for example), the other balls will get out of synchronization and fall to the ground. On the other hand (sorry!), if you neglect a ball by keeping it in your hand too short a time, the balls will again get out of sync and come crashing to the ground.

Effective juggling of life roles means giving appropriate attention to each role while keeping all of them in an overall rhythm. This rhythm provides the foundation for maximizing each life role. Once you achieve a rhythmical juggling of your life roles, you will find it easy to control each while keeping them all in order. When you achieve this, you will discover that you expend much less overall energy than if all of your life roles are fragmented.

So use the concept of juggling to gain a broader perspective in taking care of yourself. You may want to learn how to juggle so that you can actually experience what I am talking about. Just please don't try to juggle forty-five-pound plates!

Giving Something Back

There seems to be one subtle quality that distinguishes a warrior bodybuilder from others. This quality is one's willingness to help others. It is almost as if warrior bodybuilders have some kind of duty or obligation to give something back to the sport they love. So these people share their knowledge and experience to help others accelerate their progress.

One thing that I have been struck with when meeting top bodybuilders is their openness to take time out and help others. Sure, during a workout or the month preceding a competition, they shouldn't be disturbed, but after the workout or the competition these bodybuilders frequently bend over backwards to help others.

Many of these warriors feel an obligation to help others. They say that people helped them on their way up, so they have the duty to pass it on. They want others to avoid the same mistakes they made, as well as maximize what they have found to be effective.

Hence, one of the important roles of a warrior bodybuilder is that

of teacher, guide, partner, confidant, or coach. This does not mean that they are over-the-hill as bodybuilders. On the contrary, giving something back to the sport adds an extra dimension to their bodybuilding. By doing so, the warrior bodybuilder often gains a whole new respect and appreciation for the sport.

Bodybuilding has progressed by leaps and bounds over the last twenty years. Much of this accelerated progress can be attributed to warrior bodybuilders in every gym sharing their wisdom with others. By helping each other we help our sport and, in the long run, help ourselves.

The bodybuilding lifestyle is a committed and purposeful one that is balanced by attending to all of life's roles and giving something back to the sport. This complete picture keeps our whole lives and the sport developing as much as our bodies.

Frontiers

The bodybuilding warrior is continually asking him- or herself, "Where do I go from here?" Warriors are always searching for new methods, techniques, and approaches to test and expand themselves. They look at their development as a challenge and establish goals accordingly to keep themselves striving. How we approach our future in sculpting our bodies greatly determines what we will become. Warriors understand this and continually view their future in what they call frontiers, whereas other bodybuilders continually view their future in terms of limitations.

You see, our underlying beliefs about ourselves and our pursuits greatly affect—for better or for worse—our attitudes in any situation we encounter. For example, if I sincerely believe the heaviest weight I can bench-press for quality reps is 295 pounds, then no matter how strong and developed I become, I will never surpass this level.

In order for you to consistently improve in your training (as well as in the other areas of your life), you will have to change your belief systems away from your limitations—focusing on what you cannot do—to the concept I call frontiers—focusing on what you *can do*. Whereas the notion of limitations connotes to me images of barriers, walls, and roadblocks, the notion of frontiers makes me think of measuring posts, signposts, and even springboards. This distinction is much more than a semantic exercise. Believing in your frontiers kicks in a whole different set of attitudes, drives, and energies that can drastically facilitate your training. Top bodybuilders view their training frontiers in terms of, "This is how far I've gone before. Let's see just how far beyond this I can go today."

If you take the time to listen to conversations in the gym, you will hear a lot of excuses, complaints, and just sheer self-put-downs. Most of these serve only to defend and even strengthen self-imposed limitations. Here are some of the more creative cop-outs I have heard lately: "Boy, it's simply impossible for me to perform six sets of leg extensions, so why should I even try?" "You see, I have this old football injury. . . ." "My training partner grunts so loud that it breaks my concentration." "I've been weak on my pull-ups because I've always been so tall that my feet touched the floor." "My small bone structure prevents me from doing any hard barbell curls." And my personal favorite, "My biorhythms are all on critical days today!"

Presented in this way, it is obvious just how absurd such statements are, but many people really believe them. If these people spent that energy and creativity believing in themselves and testing how far they could go instead of arguing for and defending their self-imposed limitations, they would soon make unbelievable (for them) progress.

The longer I am on this earth, the more aware I become that most of my limitations are self-imposed. Richard Bach, that wonderful writer who has produced many fine works including *Jonathan Livingston Seagull*, *Illusions*, and *The Bridge Across Forever*, said in that second book, "Argue for your limitations and, sure enough, they're yours." Think about this passage for a while. How many people do you know (possibly including yourself) who spend enormous amounts of time and energy defending their self-imposed limitations?

Transforming your belief systems into terms of growth, improvement, realistic optimism, and frontiers is essential for limitless bodybuilding. This is the challenge of the warrior. Sure, I cannot jump over a tall building in a single bound . . . yet! But if I keep telling myself there is no way in the world I can ever reach the top of the building, I will never find the stairs. You will never know how far you can go, or what you can become, until you believe in yourself and give yourself a chance to find out.

I know, it is very easy for me to say "think positive" and "believe in yourself," but in the long run there is really nothing else you can do. Being negative will allow you to become only a mediocre bodybuilder. The important thing to remember is that you strengthen whatever beliefs you hold—either your self-imposed limitations or your frontiers. *Build upon what you are and can do, instead of what you are not and cannot do.* This is the secret to consistent bodybuilding improvement.

The great inspirational author Napoleon Hill wrote something that has evolved into one of my basic tenets of life. He said, "Whatever can be conceived and believed can be achieved." It is as simple and profound as that. Open your mind to the possibilities of what you can become, trust yourself, and then go out and do it!

Bodybuilding warriors know it takes a lot more courage to be positive and to continually push themselves to their personal frontiers. They face the fear of the unknown and, paraphrasing the prologue from the old *Star Trek* television series, they boldly go where they haven't gone before.

This is the mandate of the bodybuilding warrior.

The Warrior's Code

Modern-day warriors are examples of the best that can be achieved through bodybuilding. You don't have to be an advanced body-

builder or a Mr. or Ms. Olympia contender to be a warrior, but you must possess the personal qualities characterized by the following guidelines. These guidelines can be thought of as the warrior's code, a summary of the things you need to be in order to become the best possible you.

1. *Warriors are disciplined people who are committed to excellence.* Warriors are dedicated to bodybuilding and give it a priority in their daily lives. They are not afraid to dream or to aspire, but they go the extra step in putting these thoughts into specific, appropriate, and attainable goals and plans.

2. *Warriors are positive people.* Warriors know that in approaching any situation they really have only two options: to be positive or to be negative. They actively choose to be positive—to realistically build themselves up and approach every situation with a "can do" attitude. Warriors assert active control over their lives by believing and trusting in themselves. They know that they not only must be positive, they must also exude this positiveness. Right thinking must be coupled with right action.

3. *Warriors view training sessions as personal proving grounds.* They approach their training as the ancient warriors approached their battles, but modern-day warriors do not battle anyone.

They do not even battle the weights. Their goal is to join with the weights to become the best they can. Their challenge is to battle their fears, doubts, and insecurities. Bodybuilding warriors are purposeful people who concentrate fully and imaginatively on the tasks at hand. They focus on churning out quality sets with proper form. They feel an inner sense of satisfaction in training the proper way.

4. *Warriors are persistent*. They know that they are involved in their training for the long run. Warriors value and even cherish their striving and struggling. They endure discomfort knowing that this is precisely the time when they are best extending themselves physically as well as mentally. They continually push themselves to their own frontiers of growth and development. Warriors accept and learn from their failures and disappointments to become better at what they do. Warriors are always willing to keep on learning and expanding themselves. They are involved in pumping iron "for life."

5. *Warriors live a balanced life*. They know that in order to consistently put in quality workouts, they must have the rest of their lives in order. They have integrated their beliefs and practices into every area of their lives so they are consistent and congruent. They have learned how to juggle their life roles in order to give each attention while maintaining an overall rhythm. Being a warrior means being a warrior in all aspects of one's life.

6. *Finally, warriors serve others*. These people understand that part of their duty is to give something back by helping others. They teach and assist so others can maximize their own progress. In a way, warriors serve as role models so that the novice and intermediate bodybuilders can eventually also become warriors. By continually sharing their knowledge and experience, warriors also advance the sport they love.

This code of the bodybuilding warrior, I propose to you, is meant to be a challenge. Do not blindly accept or reject it, but expand upon it to develop your own standards of bodybuilding excellence.

Take a couple of minutes and assess your qualifications for becoming a bodybuilding warrior by answering these questions:

- Am I dedicated to building the best body I can?   **yes   no**

- Do I have realistic, appropriate, and attainable goals? **yes no**
- Do I strive to make each workout better than the last? **yes no**
- Do I follow the principle that whatever I can conceive and believe I can achieve? **yes no**
- Have I integrated my workout life with the rest of my life? **yes no**
- Have I learned how to juggle the fitness portion of my life with my relationships, my career or education, and the spiritual portion of my life? **yes no**
- Am I persistent in striving toward my goals? Do I endure when the going gets tough? **yes no**
- Do I help others and give something back to the sport? **yes no**
- Do I regularly focus on my frontiers of development instead of my limitations? **yes no**
- Am I always open to learning something new? **yes no**
- Do I genuinely enjoy what I do? **yes no**

If you answered "yes" to these questions, you are well on your way to being a true bodybuilding warrior. Be honest with yourself and assess those areas you need to work on. Much of the courage to do something emanates from the honesty of self-awareness.

The main points I learned—or was reminded of—from this chapter were:

1. _____ .
2. _____ .
3. _____ .
4. _____ .

What is the one point I will apply or practice during the next forty-eight hours (list the days here: _____

_____)

during my workouts? _____

_____ .

Finally, what is my personal code for living the life of a body-building warrior?

_____

_____

_____

_____

_____

_____

You may want to copy this code and put it in your wallet, purse, or training log. Refer to it often.

Bodybuilding is a wonderful sport. It fulfills a variety of needs. Sure, it develops the body. But it also develops the mind and refines the character.

It is up to you to make out of bodybuilding whatever you choose.

Epilogue

I hope you now have a better understanding of the role of the mind in bodybuilding. I have shared with you views and perspectives as well as some specific skills and techniques in better applying your mind to your training. Some of you may already be asking yourselves, "Okay, now what do I do with all of this?"

All of this new knowledge needs to be applied to your training as well as to the rest of your life. Use, experiment, and refine these tools. Like your muscles, these psychological skills need to be exercised in order to be honed to a fine edge. If they are not used, they will atrophy and eventually be forgotten. As the old saying goes, "Use it or lose it!"

Keep on breaking down and applying these skills in small, manageable parts. Go back through your notes, self-assessments, and checklists at the end of the chapters and pick out one approach or skill you wish to practice. And then do it right now!

We all have dreams and goals in our bodybuilding. The challenge is to transform these dreams and goals into reality. One old saying goes, "Talk is cheap." To that I would like to add, "but doing is proving." The only way you will prove to yourself what kind of body you can develop is to go out and do it. This is the real challenge that keeps all of us going back to the gym week in and week out.

We all have our personal paths up the mountain of bodybuilding development. Chart your path and stay on course. Believe in and trust yourself. And enjoy the trip!

Happy trails and I'll see you in the gym.

Appendix
The Psychological Components of the Weider Training System

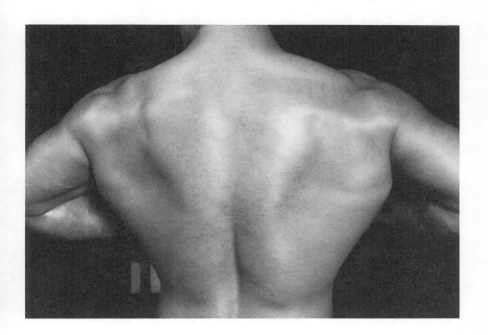

*M*uch of the development of the science of bodybuilding can be attributed to the work of Joe Weider (1981; 1984). He and his staff at the Weider Research Clinic have developed over the years a variety of proven training principles that have accelerated both the popularity and the science of bodybuilding. These training principles have demystified and simplified training techniques, cutting through the confusion, misconceptions, and just plain misinformation that used to pervade bodybuilding. The Weider Training Principles have presented systematic and sophisticated approaches that are responsible for remarkable advances in bodybuilding.

What many forget, however, is that each of these principles has an essential psychological component. Unless we emphasize the mental components, the gains from utilizing these principles will be minimized. Here, then, is a summary of the Weider Training Principles. Although some of these principles are called by different names around the world, the following are the most common names.

The *Overload Principle* is one of the basic concepts of the Weider system. This principle involves pushing yourself further with increasingly heavy weights. Approach each set with eagerness and even aggressive intensity. Really go into yourself and focus all your mental and physical energies so you will explode into the set. Remember to tune in to the muscles being worked instead of the poundage of the weight. Avoid the temptation to rush through these reps. Overloading your muscles in this way forces them to adapt. These adaptations take the form of strength, size, and endurance.

The *Muscle Priority Training Principle* proposes you perform your weakest exercises and work your weakest muscle groups early in the workout when you are more physically fresh and mentally motivated. There is a tendency to cut short or cancel entirely these exercises if you put them off to later in the workout. Be very positive and eager when approaching your weak exercises and muscle groups. Say to yourself, "Oh boy! I have a great chance to work my lagging lats now! Let's hit it!" Really believe this. View your weak exercises as exciting challenges that will bring those lagging muscles up to par with the rest of your terrific body. Chances are that if you consistently apply this principle, you will notice more profound gains in your weaker muscles than in your stronger ones.

Anxiety about lifting heavy weights, fear of failure, and discomfort frequently make us rush through a set. When we rush, we tend to swing, bounce, throw, and drop the weights. These procedures do very little good. This is why the *Slow, Continuous Training Principle* was devised. Remember, every repetition has two phases: the concentric phase and the eccentric phase. This training principle emphasizes slow and controlled movements throughout both phases of a rep. Relax, use proper form, and keep each rep slow and controlled. To aid in your control, really feel or actually become the muscles being worked. Feel how they move throughout the rep. Put it in your head that, if necessary, it will take you all day to do this particular set!

The *Iso-tension Training Principle* builds upon the previous concept by emphasizing the muscles being worked. In order to concentrate effectively, you must isolate and tune in to specific muscle groups. Focus in on the muscles being worked so well that you can feel the level of tension or contraction throughout each stage of the movement. To aid in this focus, you may want to visualize how the contracted muscles look as you feel the tension. Combining inner vision and physical sensations is a powerful adjunct to concentration.

The *Peak Contraction Training Principle* emphasizes control. The more you control your muscles throughout their full range of motion, the more you can deeply stimulate them. Remember, momentum is the enemy of muscle growth. Give priority to quality reps, not quantity reps. Contract the muscles and even exaggerate this control and contraction. In order to further accentuate this control, you may even want to visualize the muscles becoming iron or visualize the muscle fibers becoming white-hot and engorged.

The *Pyramiding Training Principle* provides you with the opportunity to gradually increase the intensity of an exercise, forcing the muscles being worked to continually adapt to new poundages with every set. With each successive set of an exercise, increase the poundage while decreasing the reps. Some bodybuilders integrate this principle into "going up and down the rack" when they go up a rack of dumbbells, increasing the weights, and immediately go back down the rack, increasing the number of reps. When you pyramid, it is important that you really concentrate and maintain form, especially during the later sets, for these are precisely the times when the muscles are forced to do their greatest adapting. Bear down and even welcome the discomfort and fatigue.

One whole series of Weider Training Principles is designed to vary and increase the intensity of your workouts. The *Superset*, *Triset*, and *Giantset Training Principles* work complementary muscle groups (such as biceps and triceps, pecs and lats, or quads and hamstrings) by immediately going from one set to another. Some advanced bodybuilders also use these principles to work the same muscle group from a couple of different angles with continuous exercises. For example, you may put in a barbell curl set and a preacher curl set back-to-back without any rest between them. This is called a *superset*. You can extend this concept to a *triset*, where you might work your triceps doing a set of pull-overs, immediately followed by a set of tricep extensions, immediately followed by a set of tricep pressdowns. *Giantsets* are four or more of such sets. Some bodybuilders even extend these principles into a circuit training workout where they immediately go from one prescribed exercise to the next. The entire six-to-ten-exercise circuit usually takes about fifteen minutes followed by a short break (or coma!). Then they start the whole circuit all over again!

These superset variations take a much longer time to complete. Even though you are lifting only about 70 percent of your normal weight in these sets, the combinations of exercises and the time duration make the difference. You will have to concentrate hard for up to four or five minutes. Plan to be as tuned in and intense during the last set as you were during the first set. Also, plan a little more rest time (but not days) between supersets. Relax, pace yourself, and convince yourself that you are in this for the long run.

All of these variations will, no doubt, send you into the discomfort zone, so program yourself that when you reach it, you will revel in the "exquisite agony" of the discomfort. Learn to actually look forward to this zone and you will soon discover that by using these superset principles you can push yourself further than you ever dreamed.

When muscles become fatigued through the course of a set, the more inner, less used muscle cells are forced to kick in to compensate for the fatiguing outer muscle cells. There is a whole series of training principles that capitalize on this process.

The first of these principles is called the *Forced Repetition Training Principle*. As you near the end of a set, with the aid of your training partner, machine, or the off hand if you are using dumbbells, force out a couple more repetitions. Become really intense and churn out the reps knowing that you are pushing these muscles further than they have ever had to go before.

A variation of forced reps is called the *Cheating Training Principle*. This principle is only for advanced bodybuilders because you will actually break form for the last couple of forced reps to get the bar back up. Cheating employs other muscle groups to lift the bar so you can extend the set a couple more reps. Use really strict form early in the set so that when you break form during the cheating, you will be able to remain safely in control. The purpose of cheating is to maximize the eccentric phase of the reps.

The third of these principles is called the *Retrogravity Training Principle*, more commonly known as negative repetitions. This principle accentuates the muscle stimulation of the eccentric, or coming down, phase of each rep. Using a training partner or the off hand, get the weight up and then very slowly resist it as it comes back down. Negative reps can be effectively used when working one appendage at a time. For example, when I am including negative reps in my leg extensions, I will do a whole set of right leg extensions. At the end of the set, I will then use my left leg to help lift the weights, remove my left leg from the bar, and let my right leg resist as I slowly come down. A couple of such negative reps at the end of a set really ignites my quads on fire!

You must plan to use these three principles intelligently in your training. Don't fall prey to the temptation to use forced reps, cheating, and negative reps on every muscle group in every workout. You are just inviting injuries. These training principles really extend the muscles beyond what they are used to, so give the muscles time to recuperate. Using one of these principles every other or every third time you work a particular muscle group is a safe and effective way to employ them.

These three principles also force your mind to endure more. Dedicate yourself to getting through these last couple of reps. Avoid saying, "Well, this is just too painful. I'll cut this short now and do an extra set." Enduring through these last couple of reps is actually better for your muscles than doing a whole extra set. Again, convince yourself to look forward to the discomfort zone, taking pride that you have the courage to really push yourself.

The *Muscle Confusion Training Principle* focuses on adding variety to your workouts. Sometimes our training routines become so routine that our muscles know what to expect. And when they know what to expect, they do not grow as fast. This principle is designed to keep your training fresh and your muscles continually adapting to variations in your training. Vary your workouts by the types of exercises, sequences, cycles, poundages, sets, rests between sets, and training principles used. You really have to plan your workouts. This is where maintaining a detailed training log becomes a valuable aid in planning each workout because you have a record of what specifically you have done in the past. You can then use this knowledge to organize each new workout to shock and surprise your muscles. Ideally, you would like to approach every one of your training sessions with the attitude, "My muscles have no idea what I have in store for them today!"

The *Holistic Training Principle* extends the notion of muscle confusion by involving you in other fitness activities. For another kind of workout or just for recreation, regularly engage in other activities such as running, bicycling, rowing, aerobics, swimming, tennis, racquetball, basketball, or cross-country skiing. These activities not only work your muscles in different ways (that is, from different angles for longer periods of time), they allow your mind to become refreshed so that you can again attack your bodybuilding. Holism proposes that the whole is greater than the sum of the individual parts. By participating in other such activities, your entire body will reflect the benefits of a fitness lifestyle.

All of these principles are grounded on the *Quality Training Principle*. As the name implies, always give priority to putting in quality efforts. Avoid the temptation to show off or train excessively. Never ever sacrifice quality for quantity. Always emphasize intelligent planning, concentrating, and maintaining proper form and control. These are the qualities necessary for consistent progress.

For many, the *Instinctive Training Principle* is the heart and soul of their training. It is nice to plan each workout, but you must also have the awareness and flexibility to adjust your routines. Our bodies continually send us signals and we have to learn to listen to these signals and act accordingly. Most great bodybuilders have said that no two of their workouts have ever been the same. The Instinctive Training Principle is based on relaxation. The more relaxed you are, the more receptive you will be to the signals from your body. Using this principle your training will actually become a harmonizing of your plans with the signals you receive from your body. This combination will allow you to maximize both the science and the art of bodybuilding.

No longer is bodybuilding a hit-and-miss activity of mindlessly pumping iron. Intelligently employing the Weider Training Principles will make your training both more efficient and effective, so that someday your reality will match your dreams.

Suggested Readings

*T*he following sources provide the best information on the psychology of bodybuilding. Some of these books present excellent information on bodybuilding routines, nutrition, and competition. Others relate indirectly to bodybuilding. The mindful bodybuilding warrior is always open to learning from a variety of sources. So pick them up and read them!

Darden, E. (1984). *High intensity bodybuilding*. New York: Perigee.

Denie. (1984). *Psycho-blast*. Brampton, Ontario, Canada: Health Culture.

DeVore, S., DeVore, G.R., & Michaelson, M. (1981). *Sybervision*. Van Nuys, CA: Delta.

Ferrigno, L. (1980). *The mind*. Marina Del Rey, CA: Dingman.

Gironda, V., & Kennedy, R. (1984). *Unleashing the wild physique*. New York: Sterling.

Hatfield, F.C., (1984). *Bodybuilding: A scientific approach*. Chicago: Contemporary Books.

Kennedy, R. (1983a). *Beef it!* New York: Sterling.

Kennedy, R. (1983b). *Hardcore bodybuilding*. New York: Sterling.

Kennedy, R. (1985). *Reps!* New York: Sterling.

Kubistant, T.M. (1984a, January). Daring to dream. *Musclemag International*, pp. 12–13, 70–71.

Kubistant, T.M. (1984b, August). The psychology of peaking. *Muscle and Fitness*, pp. 111, 211, 213, 214, 216, 219.

Kubistant, T.M. (1984c). You can talk yourself into muscle gains. In *The best of Joe Weider's muscle and fitness: Chest and shoulders*. Chicago: Contemporary Books.

Kubistant, T.M. (1985). The psychology of bodybuilding super-feature. *Muscle and Fitness,* **46** (7), 77, 93, 187–190, 192, 194–198, 202, 205–206, 208, 217–218, 221.

Kubistant, T.M. (1986). *Performing your best.* Champaign, IL: Life Enhancement Publications.

McCluggage, D. (1977). *The centered skier.* New York: Warner.

Reynolds, B., Grymkowski, R., Connors, E., & Kimber, T. (1985). *Solid gold.* Chicago: Contemporary Books.

Schwarzenegger, A. (1985). *Encyclopedia of bodybuilding.* New York: Simon and Schuster.

Schwarzenegger, A., & Hull, D.K. (1977). *Arnold: The education of a bodybuilder.* New York: Simon and Schuster.

Sybervision Systems. (1985). *The neuropsychology of achievement audio-tape series.* Newark, CA: Author.

Weider, J. (1981). *Bodybuilding: The Weider approach.* Chicago: Contemporary Books.

Weider, J., & Reynolds, B. (1984). *Competitive bodybuilding.* Chicago: Contemporary Books.

Index

About the Author

Asport psychologist and feature writer for *Muscle & Fitness*, *MuscleMag International*, and *Workout* magazines, Tom Kubistant is a highly respected authority on the psychology of bodybuilding. He contributed chapters on mental training to *The Best of Joe Weider's Muscle & Fitness* and *The Weider System* and is the author of *Performing Your Best*, published by Life Enhancement Publications. Dr. Kubistant is president of Performance and Productivity Specialists, a firm that trains and consults with athletes, performing artists, and business people.

Tom works with bodybuilders at all levels to help them get the most out of their workouts and prepare for competition. Tom also regularly works with a diversity of performers ranging from golfers, tennis players, and dancers to motocross racers and tournament poker players.

Tom has made over 1,000 presentations to community, business, professional, and school groups across the country. As director of PROVOICES, a national speakers bureau that serves conventions, conferences, seminars, retreats, and sales meetings, Tom has addressed or trained for such organizations as General Motors, Echo Bay Gold Mines, Nevada National Bank, Ford Truck Division, Surgitek Medical Engineering, and the Wisconsin Credit Union League. Tom earned his doctorate degree in counseling from Northern Illinois University in 1977.

Tom is a regular bodybuilder and runner, who always finds time for his golfing and flyfishing. He enjoys spending time with his family and helping people become successful.